Suggested Rules of Procedure for a City Council

Fourth Edition

Trey Allen

🏛 UNC | **SCHOOL OF GOVERNMENT**

The School of Government at the University of North Carolina at Chapel Hill works to improve the lives of North Carolinians by engaging in practical scholarship that helps public officials and citizens understand and improve state and local government. Established in 1931 as the Institute of Government, the School provides educational, advisory, and research services for state and local governments. The School of Government is also home to a nationally ranked Master of Public Administration program, the North Carolina Judicial College, and specialized centers focused on community and economic development, information technology, and environmental finance.

As the largest university-based local government training, advisory, and research organization in the United States, the School of Government offers up to 200 courses, webinars, and specialized conferences for more than 12,000 public officials each year. In addition, faculty members annually publish approximately 50 books, manuals, reports, articles, bulletins, and other print and online content related to state and local government. The School also produces the *Daily Bulletin Online* each day the General Assembly is in session, reporting on activities for members of the legislature and others who need to follow the course of legislation.

Operating support for the School of Government's programs and activities comes from many sources, including state appropriations, local government membership dues, private contributions, publication sales, course fees, and service contracts.

Visit sog.unc.edu or call 919.966.5381 for more information on the School's courses, publications, programs, and services.

Michael R. Smith, DEAN
Thomas H. Thornburg, SENIOR ASSOCIATE DEAN
Frayda S. Bluestein, ASSOCIATE DEAN FOR FACULTY DEVELOPMENT
Johnny Burleson, ASSOCIATE DEAN FOR DEVELOPMENT
Michael Vollmer, ASSOCIATE DEAN FOR ADMINISTRATION
Linda H. Weiner, ASSOCIATE DEAN FOR OPERATIONS
Janet Holston, DIRECTOR OF STRATEGY AND INNOVATION

FACULTY

Whitney Afonso	Cheryl Daniels Howell	LaToya B. Powell
Trey Allen	Jeffrey A. Hughes	William C. Rivenbark
Gregory S. Allison	Willow S. Jacobson	Dale J. Roenigk
David N. Ammons	Robert P. Joyce	John Rubin
Ann M. Anderson	Diane M. Juffras	Jessica Smith
Maureen Berner	Dona G. Lewandowski	Meredith Smith
Mark F. Botts	Adam Lovelady	Carl W. Stenberg III
Anita R. Brown-Graham	James M. Markham	John B. Stephens
Peg Carlson	Christopher B. McLaughlin	Charles Szypszak
Leisha DeHart-Davis	Kara A. Millonzi	Shannon H. Tufts
Shea Riggsbee Denning	Jill D. Moore	Vaughn Mamlin Upshaw
Sara DePasquale	Jonathan Q. Morgan	Aimee N. Wall
James C. Drennan	Ricardo S. Morse	Jeffrey B. Welty
Richard D. Ducker	C. Tyler Mulligan	Richard B. Whisnant
Robert L. Farb	Kimberly L. Nelson	
Norma Houston	David W. Owens	

Printed in the United States of America

28 27 26 25 24   7 8 9 10 11

ISBN 978-1-56011-894-7

About the Series

Local Government Board Builders offers local elected leaders practical advice on how to effectively lead and govern. Each of the booklets in this series provides a topic overview, and many offer specific tips on effective practice, worksheets, and reflection questions to help local elected leaders improve their work. The series focuses on common activities for local governing boards, such as selecting and appointing committees and advisory boards, planning for the future, making better decisions, improving board accountability, and effectively engaging stakeholders in public decisions.

Vaughn Mamlin Upshaw, formerly lecturer in public administration and government at the UNC School of Government, is founding editor of the series.

Other Books in This Series

Leading Your Governing Board: A Guide for Mayors and County Board Chairs, Vaughn Mamlin Upshaw, 2009

A Model Code of Ethics for North Carolina Local Elected Officials, A. Fleming Bell, II, 2010

Creating and Maintaining Effective Local Government Citizen Advisory Committees, Vaughn Mamlin Upshaw, 2010

Working with Nonprofit Organizations, Margaret Henderson, Lydian Altman, Suzanne Julian, Gordon P. Whitaker, and Eileen R. Youens, 2010

Public Outreach and Participation, John B. Stephens, Ricardo S. Morse, and Kelley T. O'Brien, 2011

Local Government Revenue Sources in North Carolina, Kara A. Millonzi, 2011

Getting the Right Fit: The Governing Board's Role in Hiring a Manager, Vaughn Mamlin Upshaw, John A. Rible IV, and Carl W. Stenberg, 2011

The Property Tax in North Carolina, Christopher B. McLaughlin, 2012

Local Government Budgeting: A Guide for North Carolina Elected Officials, Julie M. Brenman with Gregory S. Allison, 2013

Handbook for North Carolina Mayors and Council Members, David M. Lawrence, 2013

How Are We Doing? Evaluating Manager and Board Performance, Vaughn Mamlin Upshaw, 2014

Wicked Problems: What Can Local Governments Do? Eric M. Reese and Maureen M. Berner, 2014

Strategic Planning for Elected Officials: Setting Priorities, Lydian Altman, Margaret Henderson, and Vaughn Mamlin Upshaw, 2017

Suggested Rules of Procedure for the Board of County Commissioners, Joseph S. Ferrell, Third Edition, 2002

Suggested Rules of Procedure for Small Local Government Boards, A. Fleming Bell, II, Second Edition, 1998

Suggested Rules of Procedure for a City Council, A. Fleming Bell, II, Third Edition, 2000

Contents

Preface   *vii*

Introduction   *1*

Suggested Rules of Procedure   *5*

Part I. Applicability   *5*

Rule 1. Applicability of Rules   *5*

Part II. Quorum   *6*

Rule 2. Quorum   *6*

Part III. Open Meetings   *9*

Rule 3. Remote Participation in Council Meetings   *9*

Rule 4. Meetings to Be Open to the Public   *9*

Rule 5. Closed Sessions   *10*

Rule 6. Meeting Minutes   *14*

Rule 7. Broadcasting and Recording Meetings   *17*

Part IV. Organization of the Council   *18*

Rule 8. Organizational Meeting; Selection of [Mayor and] Mayor Pro Tempore   *18*

Part V. Types of Meetings   *22*

Rule 9. Regular Meetings   *22*

Rule 10. Special Meetings   *22*

Rule 11. Emergency Meetings   *25*

Rule 12. Recessed Meetings   *26*

Part VI. Agenda   *27*

Rule 13. Agenda   *27*

Rule 14. Acting by Reference to Agenda or Other Document   *32*

Rule 15. Agenda Items from Members of the Public   *32*

Rule 16. Order of Business   *33*

Part VII. Role of the Presiding Officer   34

    Rule 17. The Mayor   *34*

    Rule 18. The Mayor Pro Tempore   *36*

    Rule 19. Other Presiding Officer   *36*

    Rule 20. When the Presiding Officer Is Active in Debate   *37*

Part VIII. Motions and Voting   37

    Rule 21. Action by the Council   *37*

    Rule 22. Second Not Required   *38*

    Rule 23. One Motion at a Time   *39*

    Rule 24. Withdrawal of Motion   *39*

    Rule 25. Debate   *40*

    Rule 26. Adoption by Majority Vote   *40*

    Rule 27. Changing a Vote   *41*

    Rule 28. Duty to Vote   *41*

    Rule 29. Voting by Written Ballot   *44*

    Rule 30. Substantive Motions   *44*

    Rule 31. Procedural Motions   *45*

Part IX. Ordinances and Contracts   57

    Rule 32. Introduction of Ordinances   *57*

    Rule 33. Adoption, Amendment, and Repeal of Ordinances   *58*

    Rule 34. Adoption of the Budget Ordinance   *61*

    Rule 35. Approval of Contracts and Authorization of Expenditures   *62*

Part X. Public Hearings and Comment Periods   63

    Rule 36. Public Hearings   *63*

    Rule 37. Public Comment Periods   *66*

Part XI. Appointments and Appointed Bodies   67

    Rule 38. Appointments   *67*

    Rule 39. Committees and Boards   *69*

Part XII. Miscellaneous   71

    Rule 40. Amendment of the Rules   *71*

    Rule 41. Reference to *Robert's Rules of Order Newly Revised*   *71*

Appendix A. Quorum for a City Council   *73*

Appendix B. Order of Precedence for Procedural Motions   *74*

Appendix C. Number of Votes Required to Adopt an Ordinance or Approve a Contract   *76*

Appendix D. N.C. City Council Procedures: Selected Statutes   *79*

Preface

This fourth edition of *Suggested Rules of Procedure for a City Council* builds on the work of Bonnie E. Davis, who authored the first edition published in 1978, and A. Fleming Bell, II, who revised and expanded the work in 1986 and again in 2000. As originally conceived, the book was an adaptation of *Robert's Rules of Order* to suit the needs of municipal governing boards. With its focus on large assemblies, *Robert's* is not always the ideal parliamentary authority for small bodies. The length of *Robert's*—the current edition exceeds 700 pages—and the number and complexity of its rules create significant potential for confusion. The small size of city councils and the lack of trained parliamentarians at most council meetings make a shorter and less complicated set of model rules desirable. Moreover, the procedural rules followed by a city council must take into account statutory requirements that go beyond or differ from *Robert's*.

Prior editions of *Suggested Rules of Procedure for a City Council* succeeded admirably in furnishing city councils with sample rules, manageable both in number and complexity, that satisfied both generally accepted parliamentary principles and the procedural requirements of state law. The commentary included in those editions discussed issues involving the application of the rules and directed the reader's attention to pertinent statutes. Councils throughout the state recognized the value of prior editions by modeling their own procedural rules on them.

Important statutory changes occurring since the publication of the third edition in 2000 have made a fourth edition necessary. One such change concerns the voting rules for city councils. Section 160A-75 of the North Carolina General Statutes (hereinafter G.S.) has long dictated that a council member's unexcused failure to vote be recorded as a vote in the affirmative. In 2015, the General Assembly amended G.S. 160A-75 to exempt from this requirement votes on whether to amend or repeal zoning ordinances. That statutory change is one of many this edition takes into account.

Yet this fourth edition is more than a mere update of the third edition to conform to changes in state law. Rules have been reordered and categorized expressly by topic. Extensive modifications have been made to the text of rules and to the explanatory comments that follow them. New rules have been added, and some rules from prior editions have been eliminated, combined with other rules, or divided into separate rules.

Two primary goals underlay the bulk of the revisions. The first was to make the rules easier to understand and apply whenever possible. This edition's approach to quorum calculations represents one attempt to achieve that goal. To determine whether a quorum of its members is present, a council must employ the calculation method prescribed in G.S. 160A-74, the peculiar wording of which has confounded quite a few city officials and even city attorneys. In an effort to eliminate such confusion, the comment section to this edition's quorum rule (Rule 2) provides a detailed explanation of quorum calculations under the statute, complete with examples, while the table in Appendix A identifies the number of members needed for a quorum based on a council's size and total number of vacant seats. The second goal was to address recurring procedural issues not covered by prior editions. So, for instance, this edition contains rules and commentary on remote participation by members in council meetings (Rule 3) and the ability of members to change their votes (Rule 27).

Suggested Rules of Procedure for a City Council is a companion to the School of Government's *Suggested Rules of Procedure for the Board of County Commissioners*, authored by Joseph S. Ferrell. I am in the process of revising the latter work and anticipate that, when complete, the two books will agree with each other more closely, except where state law or long-standing practice dictate otherwise.

Thanks are due to three individuals with whom it has been my privilege to work at the School of Government. Norma R. Houston has been part of this edition from the outset. The volume's overall organization and specific approaches to many procedural issues owe much to her influence. Frayda S. Bluestein carefully reviewed the manuscript of this edition and provided many valuable suggestions. Last but hardly least, Fleming Bell graciously took time away from retirement to offer valuable feedback on the manuscript. Professor Bell has been a prominent authority in this state for decades on board procedures, and I was delighted by his willingness to help me as I tried to expand upon his achievements. The fourth edition is much better than it would have been without the input of these fine colleagues. Of course, I alone bear responsibility for any remaining errors.

Trey Allen
Assistant Professor of Public Law and Government
Chapel Hill
Spring 2017

Introduction

The members of a city council decide important issues of public policy. This reality can lead to difficult meetings, particularly when agenda items attract public scrutiny. The model rules in this volume are intended to help city councils reach informed decisions in an effective, efficient, orderly, courteous, and fair manner, regardless of the matter under consideration.[1] The content of these rules reflects the influence of parliamentary law, statutory procedural requirements, *Robert's Rules of Order Newly Revised* and similar manuals, and the advising that faculty members at the School of Government have done on procedural issues over the years.

Parliamentary law encompasses the "recognized rules, precedents[,] and usages of legislative bodies by which their procedure is regulated. It is that system of rules and precedents that originated in the British Parliament and . . . has been developed by legislative or deliberative bodies in this and other countries."[2] Parliamentary law has yielded a number of fundamental principles for the conduct of business by deliberative bodies.[3] With city councils in mind, some of the principles may be stated as follows:

- *The council must take only those actions that lie within its authority.* In North Carolina, local governments have only those powers conferred on them by the General Assembly.[4]

---

1. *See* American Institute of Parliamentarians Standard Code of Parliamentary Procedure (hereinafter Standard Code) 2 (2012) ("The purpose of meeting procedures is to allow members to reach informed business decisions in an effective, efficient, orderly, courteous, and fair manner.").

2. American Society of Legislative Clerks and Secretaries' Mason's Manual Revision Commission, Mason's Manual of Legislative Procedure (hereinafter Mason's Manual) § 35, at 29 (2010 ed.).

3. The fundamental principles listed in this introduction are taken primarily from pages 1–4 of Mason's Manual and pages 6–10 of Standard Code.

4. King v. Town of Chapel Hill, 367 N.C. 400, 404 (2014) ("[M]unicipalities are limited to exercising those powers 'expressly conferred' or 'necessarily implied' from enabling legislation passed by the General Assembly.").

- *The council must meet in order to act.* The powers granted to the council belong to the council as a body, not to individual members, who may not act for the council except pursuant to valid delegations of authority.
- *Members of the council are equal participants.* Each member has the right to propose motions, to debate, to vote, and to exercise any other privilege of membership. At the same time, each member is bound by reciprocal obligations, such as the duty to protect the rights of fellow members.
- *Members must receive proper notice of council meetings.* Because each member has the right to participate in meetings, members should have reasonable notice of each meeting's time, place, and purpose. This principle has been codified in statutory provisions that require member notification when the council holds a meeting that is not on its regular meeting schedule.[5]
- *A quorum is necessary for the council to act.* The default rule for most deliberative bodies is that a quorum consists of a majority of a body's members, but state law specifies the method for determining whether a quorum of the city council is present.[6]
- *There must be an opportunity for debate.* The council is a deliberative body, that is, a body of persons who meet "to discuss and determine upon common action."[7] Members cannot be expected to form collective judgments unless they can exchange information and opinions concerning issues before the council.
- *Questions must be decided by voting.* Voting is the mechanism by which the council expresses its collective will.[8]
- *A majority vote is required to take action.* Inasmuch as the council operates democratically, the will of the majority is regarded as the will of the council.[9] The term "majority vote" usually means more

---

5. Section 160A-71(b) of the North Carolina General Statutes (hereinafter "G.S.").

6. G.S. 160A-74. The provisions of this statute are incorporated into Rule 2 and discussed in the *Comment* thereto.

7. *Robert's Rules of Order Newly Revised* (hereinafter *RONR* (11th ed.)), xxix.

8. *See* STANDARD CODE 147 ("[A] vote is a formal expression of the will of the assembly.").

9. *Id.* at 135 ("[I]n an organization, the ultimate authority lies in a majority of the members when they meet to take action through majority votes. This fundamental principle of voting allows members to democratically and legitimately operate their organization.")

than half of lawful votes cast, a quorum being present; however, state law or a council's own procedures may demand larger majorities for certain actions.

- *Meetings of the council must be characterized by fairness and good faith.* Part of conducting a meeting fairly is applying the council's procedural rules consistently. The consistent application of the rules ensures that members are treated the same, whatever their viewpoints on particular issues. A member who tries to manipulate the council through fraud, trickery, or deception violates his or her obligation to act in good faith.

The above principles permeate these rules. For example, consistent with the right of members to engage in debate, Rule 31 (Motion 9) does not permit the council to entertain a motion to end debate on a pending matter until every member has had a chance to speak at least once. The requirement in Rule 26 that motions pass by majority vote recognizes the fundamental place of majority rule in deliberative bodies.

A number of these rules restate procedural requirements imposed on the city council by state law. As a public body, the council must abide by the public access, notice, and other provisions of the open meetings law.[10] The demands of the open meetings law are reflected most conspicuously in Part III (Open Meetings) and Part V (Types of Meetings) of this volume. Rule 33 comports with G.S. 160A-75, the statute governing the number of votes necessary to adopt an ordinance or take any action having the effect of an ordinance. The other points at which these rules incorporate statutory requirements are too numerous to mention here but are documented in the commentary and footnotes.

City charters—local acts by which individual cities are established—constitute another major source of procedural requirements. Inasmuch as charters differ widely from city to city, it is impossible for these rules to account for their variations. Before adopting these rules, however, the council should take care to determine whether one or more rules must be modified to comply with its charter.

Many of the specifics in these rules are not dictated by fundamental parliamentary principles or by statute. Instead, they correspond more or less to procedures recommended by *Robert's* or other prominent manuals of procedure. The council has broad discretion to modify or omit any

---

10. G.S. 143-318.9, -318.18.

provision that does not embody parliamentary law or statute, and that is not mandated by its charter, even if the variation deviates from *Robert's*.[11] For instance, the restrictions in Rule 31 on motions to reconsider—who may make them and when they may be offered—could be relaxed without violating parliamentary or state law. Similarly, although Rule 22 eliminates the practice of requiring seconds to motions, the council could substitute its own rule to the contrary.

This fourth edition of *Suggested Rules of Procedure for a City Council* also bears the imprint of countless hours that faculty members at the School of Government have spent advising local governments on procedural matters. Insights gained from that experience have influenced nearly everything about these rules, including decisions as to their organization, scope, and wording. These insights have likewise inspired features intended to improve this volume's usefulness. The commentary has been significantly expanded to address issues related to the application of these rules. Footnotes cite relevant legal and persuasive authorities. Appendices A through C make it easier to identify the number of members needed for a quorum, to navigate among procedural motions, and to calculate the votes required for ordinance adoption. Selected North Carolina General Statutes that impose procedural requirements on city councils are presented in Appendix D.

True to the School's mission of promoting good government, this volume has been prepared throughout with the aim of producing a piece of practical scholarship that will aid city council members in the performance of their important duties. With that aspiration in mind, it is fitting to close with a practical recommendation. In adopting these rules, a city council should not act by ordinance. Larger majorities are usually needed to adopt or amend ordinances than to take other actions (compare Rule 33 with Rule 26). If it puts its procedural rules into an ordinance, the council will not be able to change them unless it can satisfy the elevated vote requirements for ordinances.

---

11. *See* G.S. 160A-71(c) ("The council may adopt its own rules of procedure, not inconsistent with the city charter, general law, or generally accepted principles of parliamentary procedure.")

Suggested Rules of Procedure

Part I. Applicability

Rule 1. Applicability of Rules

These rules apply to all meetings of the [_____] City Council.[1] For purposes of these rules, a meeting of the council occurs whenever a majority of the council's members gather, whether in person or simultaneously by electronic means, to conduct hearings, deliberate, vote, or otherwise transact public business within the council's real or apparent jurisdiction. The term "majority" as used here and elsewhere in these rules means, unless otherwise specified, a simple majority, that is, more than half.

> **Comment:** A city council may adopt rules of procedure, so long as they do not conflict with its charter, general law, or generally accepted principles of parliamentary procedure.[2] The suggested rules in this volume incorporate pertinent statutory requirements, important judicial decisions on procedural issues, and general parliamentary principles. Some councils will need to modify one or more of these suggested rules to conform to provisions in their charters.
>
> The effect of Rule 1 is to make these rules applicable to any gathering of council members covered by the open meetings law,

---

1. In North Carolina, the legal status and authority of a municipality is the same, regardless of whether it is denominated a city, town, or village. *See* G.S. 160A-1(2) (defining the term "city" as used in Chapter 160A to mean "a municipal corporation . . . having the powers, duties, privileges, and immunities conferred by law on cities, towns, and villages"). The same is true of a municipal governing board, which may be known as a council, board of aldermen, or board of commissioners. *See* G.S. 160A-1(3) (noting that the term "council" as used in Chapter 160A is interchangeable with the terms "board of aldermen" and "board of commissioners"). These rules employ the term "city council" for the sake of convenience and in deference to the terminology found in Chapter 160A, the primary statutes governing municipal corporations.

2. G.S. 160A-71(c).

which imposes public notice, access, and other requirements on the official meetings of public bodies.[3] For purposes of that law and these rules, members are deemed to hold an official meeting whenever a majority of them come together in one place or gather simultaneously by electronic means to conduct public business within the council's real or apparent jurisdiction.[4] On the other hand, purely social and other informal gatherings do not qualify as meetings of the council, unless they are called or held to evade the spirit and purposes of the open meetings law.[5]

As indicated by the word "deliberate" in Rule 1, these rules extend to gatherings at which a majority of council members discuss city business, even if no action is taken.

Because of the peculiar wording of G.S. 160A-74, the quorum statute for city councils, the number of members sufficient to trigger the open meetings law may in some instances be smaller than the number necessary to constitute a quorum. See Rule 2 and the *Comment* thereto for a more detailed explanation of this point.

Part II. Quorum

Rule 2. Quorum

The presence of a quorum is necessary for the council to conduct business. A majority of the council's actual membership plus the mayor, excluding vacant seats, constitutes a quorum. A member who withdraws from a meeting without being excused by majority vote of the remaining members in attendance is deemed present for quorum purposes.

> **Comment:** This rule complies with G.S. 160A-74. In accordance with Rule 1, the term "majority" as used here should be understood to mean a simple majority, that is, more than half.[6]

---

3. G.S. 143-318.9, -318.18.

4. G.S. 143-318.10(d).

5. *Id.*

6. *See RONR* (11th ed.) 400, ll. 7–8 (noting that "[t]he word *majority* means 'more than half'").

General. The term "quorum" refers to the minimum number of members who must be present for a body to conduct business.[7] It usually does not refer to the number of members who vote on a particular motion.[8]

The mere existence of a quorum does not always mean that the council has enough members present to take a particular action. As set out in Rule 26 and the *Comment* thereto, a simple majority—more than half—of votes cast, a quorum being present, is sufficient to adopt most motions; however, some actions that may be taken by city councils are subject to larger voting requirements imposed by statute or these rules. See, for example, the voting requirements in Rule 33 for the adoption of ordinances.

Withdrawal from meeting. By stipulating that a member who withdraws from a meeting without being excused still counts as present, G.S. 160A-74 and this rule deny any single member the power to deprive the council of a quorum merely by stepping out of the council chamber.

Quorum calculations. The peculiar wording of the quorum statute has led to confusion. Some have read it quite literally to require the presence of both a majority of a council's members and the mayor for a quorum to exist. It is clear, however, that the General Assembly did not intend for the statute to be interpreted in this way. For one thing, such a literal reading of G.S. 160A-74 would effectively invalidate G.S. 160A-70, the statute that requires the council to select a mayor pro tempore. General Statute 160A-70 allows the council to confer any of the mayor's powers and duties on the mayor pro tem "[d]uring the absence of the mayor" and to "elect from its members a temporary chairman to preside" when "both the mayor and the mayor pro tempore are absent from a meeting." If there could be no quorum without the mayor, G.S. 160A-70 would be largely pointless because the mayor's absence would leave the council powerless to conduct business.

The provisions of the city quorum statute and this rule are best viewed as a math formula. The quorum for a city council consists of a majority of X. The statute and Rule 2 tell us to calculate X by adding the mayor to the council's total membership and subtracting vacant

---

7. *RONR* (11th ed.) 345, ll. 3–7.
8. *Id.*

seats. In other words, they direct us to view the mayor as part of the council for quorum purposes. This is true regardless of whether the mayor may vote on all questions or only to break a tie vote.

Suppose a five-member council has no vacancies. The quorum for the council may be calculated as follows:

$$
\begin{array}{rl}
5 & \text{(Total number of council seats)} \\
+\ 1 & \text{(mayor)} \\
-\ 0 & \text{(no vacancies)} \\
\hline
6. &
\end{array}
$$

Quorum = 4 (more than ½ of 6).

Because the mayor is treated as part of the council in quorum determinations, any four members or the mayor and any three members constitute a quorum of this hypothetical council.

The table in Appendix A is intended to simplify quorum determinations. It identifies the number needed for a quorum based on the council's size and the number of vacant seats.

Quorum and the open meetings law. The public notice and access provisions of the open meetings law apply whenever a "majority" of a public body's members gather to transact public business within the body's real or apparent jurisdiction.[9] Because the open meetings law employs the term "majority" rather than "quorum," it is sometimes possible for the law to be triggered by a gathering of council members, even when a quorum of the council is not present. Consider again the hypothetical five-member council referred to above. Although four members (or three members plus the mayor) are necessary for a quorum, the gathering of any three members to discuss city business is subject to the open meetings law because three members equal a majority of the council. If members fail to grasp this point, they might violate the open meetings law unintentionally.

Remote participation. Some councils allow members who are not physically present to take part in meetings electronically. Rule 3 and its *Comment* address the implications of this practice for quorum calculations.

---

9. G.S. 143-318.10(d).

Part III. Open Meetings[10]

Rule 3. Remote Participation in Council Meetings

No member who is not physically present for a council meeting may participate in the meeting by electronic means except in accordance with a policy adopted by the council. [Although a member who attends a meeting electronically pursuant to such a policy may take part in debate, the member may neither be counted toward a quorum nor vote on any matter before the council.]

> **Comment:** Although the open meetings law acknowledges the possibility of remote (electronic) participation by the members of public bodies,[11] no statute expressly authorizes council members who are not physically present to take part in city council meetings. Consequently, if a council elects to allow remote participation, it should spell out the conditions under which members may participate in meetings via conference call, Skype, or similar devices or applications.
>
> Given the lack of explicit statutory authority for remote participation, the city council runs the risk of having its actions invalidated if it relies on a member who is not in the meeting room to establish a quorum or to cast the deciding vote on a matter. The optional language in brackets is for councils that do not want to run that risk.[12]

Rule 4. Meetings to Be Open to the Public

Except as permitted by Rule 5, all meetings of the council shall be open to the public, and any person may attend its meetings.

> **Comment:** The presumption under the open meetings law is that a public body's meetings will be open to the public.[13] The law allows a public body to enter closed session, however, for the reasons set out in G.S. 143-318.11 and Rule 5.

---

10. The requirements of the open meetings law are examined in great detail in Frayda S. Bluestein & David M. Lawrence, Open Meetings and Local Governments in North Carolina: Some Questions and Answers (8th ed. 2017).

11. G.S. 143-318.13(a).

12. For more information about the legal issues raised by remote participation by members of public bodies, see Frayda S. Bluestein, *Remote Participation in Local Government Board Meetings*, Loc. Gov't L. Bull. 133 (Aug. 2013), www.sog.unc.edu/sites/www.sog.unc.edu/files/reports/lglb133.pdf.

13. G.S. 143-318.10(a).

Rule 5. Closed Sessions

(a) Motion to Enter Closed Session. The city council may enter a closed session from which the public is excluded only upon a motion duly made and adopted in open session. The motion to enter closed session must cite one or more of the permissible bases for closed session listed in paragraph (b) of this rule. A motion to enter closed session under subparagraph (b)(1) or (b)(2) must contain the additional information specified in those provisions.

(b) Bases for Closed Session. A closed session is permissible under the following circumstances and no others:

(1) To prevent the disclosure of information that is privileged or confidential pursuant to the law of North Carolina or of the United States or that does not constitute a public record within the meaning of Chapter 132 of the General Statutes. The motion to enter closed session must name or cite the law that renders the information confidential or privileged.

Comment: Subparagraph (b)(1) restates G.S. 143-318.11(a)(1). Chapter 132 of the General Statutes comprises the state's public records law.

This exception applies not only to records that must be withheld from public inspection because they are confidential, but also to non-confidential records that fall outside the public records law's definition of "public records." For example, under G.S. 132-1.7(a), the term "public records" does not cover security plans or detailed plans or drawings of public buildings and infrastructure facilities. The council may enter closed session to review such plans or drawings, even though their disclosure would not violate the law.

(2) To consult with the city attorney or another attorney employed or retained by the city in order to preserve the attorney–client privilege. If the council expects to discuss a pending lawsuit with its attorney, the motion to enter closed session must include the names of the parties to the lawsuit.

Comment: Subparagraph (b)(2) restates G.S. 143-318.11(a)(2). The open meetings law expressly prohibits a public body from discussing general policy matters when it goes into closed session to consult with its attorney. Additionally, the mere presence of the city attorney at a council meeting is not grounds for a closed session. Unless the council is going into closed session for the purpose of consulting with its attorney on a legal issue, it should not invoke the attorney–client privilege as a basis for closed session.

A council that enters closed session to consult with its attorney may consider and give instructions to the attorney regarding claims, litigation, and other legal proceedings brought by or against the council. If the council considers or approves a settlement in closed session, then (unless the settlement resolves malpractice claims against a public hospital) the settlement's terms must be reported to the council in open session and entered into the council's minutes as soon as possible within a reasonable time after the settlement is reached.

The handling or settlement of claims or legal proceedings is not the exclusive basis for going into closed session to preserve the attorney–client privilege. The council may enter closed session to discuss any legal issue with its attorney. This exception may be used only if the attorney is present for the closed session, either physically or by electronic means.

(3) To discuss matters relating to (a) the location or expansion of industries or other businesses in the area served by the city or (b) the closure or realignment of a military installation. The council may reach agreement in closed session on a tentative list of economic development incentives to be offered in negotiations, but the approval of the signing of any economic development contract or commitment and the authorization of the payment of economic development expenditures must take place in open session.

Comment: Subparagraph (b)(3) restates G.S. 143-318.11(a)(4).

(4) To establish or instruct staff or agents concerning the city's position in negotiating the price or other material terms of an agreement for the acquisition of real property by purchase, exchange, or lease.

Comment: Subparagraph (b)(4) restates part of G.S. 143-318.11(a)(5). If requested to do so, the council must disclose the following information before going into closed session on this basis: (a) the current owner of the property, (b) the property's location, and (c) the use to which the council intends to put the property.[14]

---

14. Boney Publishers, Inc. v. Burlington City Council, 151 N.C. App. 651, 657 (2002).

Neither G.S. 143-318.11(a)(5) nor this rule permits a closed session to discuss the sale of city property. Similarly, neither provision authorizes a closed session to discuss the purchase or lease of personal property.

(5) To establish or instruct staff or agents concerning the amount of compensation or other material terms of an employment contract.

Comment: Subparagraph (b)(5) restates part of G.S. 143-318.11(a)(5).

(6) To consider the qualifications, competence, performance, character, fitness, or conditions of appointment or employment of a public officer or employee or prospective public officer or employee, except when the individual in question is a member of the city council or other public body or is being considered to fill a vacancy on the city council or other public body. Final action to appoint or employ a public officer or employee must take place in open session.

Comment: Subparagraph (b)(6) restates part of G.S. 143-318.11(a)(6). The council may not go into closed session on this basis to consider general personnel policy issues. It likewise in most circumstances may not enter closed session to discuss a member or prospective member of the council or any of the city's appointed bodies.

(7) To hear or investigate a charge or complaint by or against a public officer or employee. Final action discharging an employee or removing an officer must occur in open session.

Comment: Subparagraph (b)(7) restates part of G.S. 143-318.11(a)(6). This basis for closed session is largely self-explanatory, except insofar as grievances against individual council members or members of appointed bodies are concerned. It might allow a council to go into closed session to hear such a grievance, but because a council member's or appointed board member's competence, performance, character, and fitness may not be considered in closed session, any discussion of the substance of the grievance and any action taken against the member in response to the grievance would probably have to take place in open session.

(8) To plan, conduct, or hear reports concerning investigations of alleged criminal misconduct.

Comment: Subparagraph (b)(8) restates G.S. 143-318.11(a)(7).

(9) To view a law enforcement recording released pursuant to G.S. 132-1.4A.

Comment: General Statute 132-1.4A sharply restricts the circumstances in which a law enforcement agency may disclose (make available for listening or viewing) or release (provide a copy) of audio and visual recordings captured by body-worn cameras, dashboard cameras, or other recording devices operated by or on behalf of the agency or its law enforcement personnel in the performance of their duties.[15] The open meetings law allows a public body to which such a recording has been released to review it in closed session.[16]

(10) On any other basis permitted by law.

Comment: Over the years, the General Assembly has expanded the list of grounds on which a public body may meet in closed session. Subparagraph (b)(10) acknowledges the possibility that this could happen again.

(c) Closed Session Participants. Unless the council directs otherwise, the city manager, city attorney, and city clerk may attend closed sessions of the council. No other person may attend a closed session unless invited by majority vote of the council.

Comment: The open meetings law does not specifically address who may attend a closed session. The typical council will usually want its manager, attorney, and clerk to be there, but the council may in its discretion exclude them, except for the attorney when the closed session is being held to preserve the attorney–client privilege. All other non-members should be excluded from closed session except when their presence is reasonably necessary to aid the council's deliberations. Note that in certain situations closed session attendance must be restricted due to the confidential nature of the matters under consideration. When, for example, the council meets in closed session to consult with its attorney, the council risks waiving the attorney–client privilege if it allows someone to attend

---

15. *See* Frayda Bluestein, *Answers to Questions About North Carolina's Body-Worn Camera Law*, Coates' Canons: NC Loc. Gov't L. Blog (July 20, 2016), http://canons.sog.unc.edu/answers-questions-north-carolinas-body-worn-camera-law/ (discussing impact of laws governing access to audio and visual recordings captured by law enforcement agencies' body-worn cameras and dashboard cameras).

16. G.S. 143-318.11(a)(10).

who is not covered by the privilege. Likewise, if the council enters closed session to examine city personnel records that are confidential under G.S. 160A-168, it must exclude anyone who is not authorized to access those records.

(d) Motion to Return to Open Session. Upon completing its closed session business, the council shall end the closed session by adopting a duly made motion to return to open session.

> **Comment:** The open meetings law does not list adjournment among the actions that a public body may take in closed session. Accordingly, the city council must return to open session following the conclusion of a closed session, even if adjournment is the only remaining item of business.

Rule 6. Meeting Minutes

(a) Minutes Required for All Meetings. The council must keep full and accurate minutes of all of its meetings, including closed sessions. To be "full and accurate," minutes must record all actions taken by the council. They should set out the precise wording of each motion and make it possible to determine the number of votes cast for and against each motion. The minutes need not record discussions of the council, though the council in its discretion may decide to incorporate such details into the minutes.

> **Comment:** Both G.S. 160A-72 and the open meetings law require a city council to keep full and accurate minutes for all of its meetings.[17] According to the North Carolina Supreme Court, minutes "should contain mainly a record of what was *done* at the meeting, not what was *said* by the members."[18] Why? Because the purpose of minutes "is to reflect matters such as motions made, the movant, points of order, and appeals—not to show discussion or absence of action."[19] Nonetheless, because the minutes belong to the council, the council may choose to record the substance of its discussions in the minutes, and many councils do just that.
>
> The minutes should make clear the total number of votes cast for and against each motion. Some actions must be approved by more

---

17. G.S. 143-318.10(e).
18. Maready v. City of Winston-Salem, 342 N.C. 708, 733 (1996) (internal quotation marks omitted) (emphases in original).
19. *Id.*

than a simple majority. If the council's adoption of a motion to take such an action were challenged on the ground that not enough members voted in favor of it, the court would examine the minutes to ascertain whether the requisite supermajority supported the motion.

Under the open meetings law, a public body's minutes "may be in written form or, at the option of the public body, may be in the form of sound or video and sound recordings."[20] Various statutory provisions in Chapter 160A, though, assume that written minutes are required for city council meetings.[21] Moreover, because the council's minutes qualify as essential government records, guidance promulgated by the Department of Natural and Cultural Resources pursuant to G.S. 132-8.2 mandates that the council, within the limitations of funds available for the purpose, create preservation duplicates of its minutes in the form of paper or microfilm copies.[22]

(b) Record of "Ayes" and "Noes." At the request of any member of the council, the minutes shall list each member by name and record how each member voted on a particular matter.

> **Comment:** Although the minutes should indicate the number of votes cast for and against every motion, the general rule is that they need not state how each member voted by name. Pursuant to G.S. 160A-72, however, the minutes must record how each member voted on a motion if any member requests that they include the "ayes" and "noes."

(c) General Accounts of Closed Sessions. In addition to minutes, the council must keep a general account of each closed session. The general account must be sufficiently detailed to provide a person not in attendance with a reasonable understanding of what transpired. The council may combine the minutes and general account of a closed session into one document, so long

---

20. G.S. 143-318.10(e).

21. *See, e.g.,* G.S. 160A-78 (calling for the council's ordinance book to be kept separate and apart from its "minute book") and -171 (directing the city clerk to "keep a journal" of the council's proceedings).

22. Government Records Section, North Carolina Department of Natural and Cultural Resources, *Public Records Requiring Human-Readable Preservation Duplicates*, www.archives.ncdcr.gov/Portals/3/PDF/gov_lists/Human_Readable_Records_Policy.pdf?ver=2016-03-11-084032-487.

as the document contains both a complete record of actions taken and the level of detail required for a general account.

> **Comment:** According to the open meetings law, "when a public body meets in closed session, it shall keep a general account of the closed session so that a person not in attendance would have a reasonable understanding of what transpired."[23] This wording plainly requires more than a mere record of actions taken. Concerns about whether the general account of a closed session is sufficiently thorough should be referred to the city attorney.
>
> As paragraph (c) recognizes, many councils incorporate the minutes and general account of a closed session into a single record. There is no legal problem with that practice, so long as the record includes any actions taken by the council in closed session and enough information about what was discussed to satisfy the statutory standard for a general account.

(d) Sealing Closed Session Records. Minutes and general accounts of closed sessions shall be sealed until unsealed by order of the council or, if the council delegates the authority to unseal to one or more staff members, in accordance with guidelines adopted by the council. The sealed minutes and general account of any closed session may be withheld from public inspection so long as public inspection would frustrate the purpose(s) of the closed session.

> **Comment:** Although the open meetings law allows a public body to withhold the minutes and general account of a closed session from public inspection for as long as necessary to avoid frustrating the purpose of the closed session,[24] the state's public records law presumes that documents made or received in the transaction of public business must be made available for inspection and copying. The council therefore should not assume that closed session records are automatically sealed without action on its part.[25] By adopting paragraph (d), the council decides that all of its closed session records will be sealed initially and remain so until they are unsealed by the council or by staff members to whom the council has delegated the

---

23. G.S. 143-318.10(e).
24. *Id.*
25. *See* David M. Lawrence, Public Records Law for North Carolina Local Governments 350 (2d ed. 2009).

authority to make such determinations pursuant to certain guidelines. Staff persons who are entrusted with the responsibility of reviewing and unsealing closed session records typically include the city attorney, the city manager or administrator, the city clerk, or some combination thereof.

The council's guidance to staff members on unsealing closed session records should probably direct them to review those records at regular intervals and unseal them as appropriate, even when no request to inspect or copy the records is pending.[26] Such periodic reviews can reduce the likelihood that closed session records will impermissibly remain under seal beyond the point at which their release would no longer frustrate the purpose(s) for which the council entered closed session.

Rule 7. Broadcasting and Recording Meetings

(a) Right to Broadcast and Record. Any person may photograph, film, tape-record, or otherwise reproduce any part of a council meeting that must take place in open session. Except as provided in paragraph (c) of this rule, any radio or television station may broadcast any such part of a council meeting.

> **Comment:** Paragraph (a) restates G.S. 143-318.14(a).

(b) Advance Notice. Any radio or television station that plans to broadcast any portion of a council meeting shall so notify the [city clerk/city manager/administrator] no later than [twenty-four hours] before the meeting. The failure to provide notice is not, by itself, grounds for preventing the broadcast of a council meeting.

> **Comment:** Paragraph (b) assumes that, if provided with advance notice of a broadcast media organization's intent to cover a council meeting, city staff will be better able to accommodate the organization and minimize any interference with the meeting. The last sentence in paragraph (b) acknowledges that neither the council nor its staff has any statutory authority to exclude broadcast media for failing to give the prescribed notice.

(c) Equipment Placement. The [city manager/administrator] may regulate the placement and use of camera or recording equipment in order to prevent undue interference with a council meeting, so long as he or she allows the

---

26. *Id.*

equipment to be placed where it can carry out its intended function. If the [city manager/administrator] determines in good faith that the equipment and personnel necessary to broadcast, photograph, or record the meeting cannot be accommodated without undue interference to the meeting, and an adequate alternative meeting room is not readily available, the [city manager/administrator] may require the pooling of the equipment and the personnel operating it.

> **Comment:** The open meetings law vests the powers set out in paragraph (c) in the council.[27] Paragraph (c) delegates these powers to the city manager or administrator, primarily because, unlike the council, the city manager or administrator may act outside of and in advance of a meeting.
>
> The open meetings law specifies that a public body may not classify the ordinary use of camera or recording equipment as an undue interference with its meeting.[28]

(d) Alternative Meeting Site. If the news media request an alternative meeting site to accommodate news coverage, and the council grants the request, the news media making the request shall pay the costs incurred by the city in securing an alternative meeting site.

> **Comment:** Paragraph (d) is taken from G.S. 143-318.14(b).

Part IV. Organization of the Council

Rule 8. Organizational Meeting; Selection of [Mayor and] Mayor Pro Tempore

(a) Scheduling Organizational Meeting. The council must hold an organizational meeting following each general election in which council members are elected. The organizational meeting must be held either (1) on the date and at the time of the council's first regular meeting in December following the election or (2) at an earlier date, if any, set by the incumbent council.

---

27. *See* G.S. 143-318.14(b).
28. *Id.*

The organizational meeting may not be held before municipal election results are officially determined, certified, and published as required by law.

Comment: This provision tracks the requirements of G.S. 160A-68(a). The statutes governing the certification and publication of election results reside in Subchapter IX of Chapter 163 of the General Statutes.

The default statutory rule is that the organizational meeting is held at council's first regular meeting in December after municipal election results have been properly certified and published under the state's election laws. The incumbent council may schedule the organizational meeting for an earlier date and time, provided the meeting occurs after the certification and publication of election results.

Neither state law nor these rules designate who should preside at the organizational meeting until the new mayor takes the oath of office. Local customs differ on this point. In some cities the city clerk, manager, or attorney presides temporarily, while in others the outgoing mayor wields the gavel until relieved by his or her successor.

The organizational meeting is often one part of a longer council meeting. The standard practice in some cities is to place the organizational meeting on the agenda under new business, leaving the incumbent council free to take up old business before the incoming members are sworn. This rule does not prohibit that practice; however, if the organizational meeting is delayed until the council's first regular meeting in December, the law may require that the organizational meeting be the first item of business. In such circumstances, G.S. 160A-68(a) stipulates that the organizational meeting must occur "on the date *and at the time*" of the regular meeting. (Emphasis added.)

If the incumbent council wants to hold the organizational meeting at its first regular meeting in December but also wishes to act on unfinished business before the incoming members join the council, it can accomplish this objective by

- recessing its November regular meeting until some date/time prior to the December regular meeting or
- scheduling a special meeting for a date/time prior to the December regular meeting.

(b) Oath of Office. As the first order of business at the organizational meeting, all newly elected members of the council must take and subscribe the oath of office set out in Article VI, Section 7, of the North Carolina Constitution. Each member's oath must be filed with the city clerk. Although a member who is not present for the organizational meeting may take the oath of office at another time, every member must take, subscribe, and file the oath before he or she begins performing any of the duties of the member's office.

> **Comment:** Article VI, Section 7, of the North Carolina Constitution expressly requires all public officers to take and subscribe the oath of office prescribed therein before they take up the duties of their offices. (An official subscribes the oath by signing beneath it.) Subsection (b) of G.S. 160A-68 echoes this requirement by directing all newly elected mayors and council members to take that oath at the organizational meeting.
>
> Additionally, G.S. 11-7 sets out an oath of office that all state and local elected and appointed officials must take and subscribe before they enter into or take up the duties of their offices. The oath is substantially similar to the oath in Article VI, Section 7, however, and decisions from the North Carolina Supreme Court and the North Carolina Court of Appeals strongly imply that taking either of them is equivalent to taking the other.[29]
>
> It stands to reason that a newly elected member who is unable to attend the organizational meeting may take the oath of office at another time. Subsection (b) of G.S. 160A-68 seems to contemplate that possibility by declaring that, provided a quorum is present, the organizational meeting must take place despite the absence, death, or refusal to serve of any member(s). Moreover, an incoming member's failure to attend the organizational meeting in no way invalidates the election results. It should be noted, though, that ordinarily the incumbent member will remain in office until the incoming member takes and subscribes the oath.[30]
>
> Only certain officials may administer the oath of office.[31] They include, among others, the mayor, the city clerk, and a notary public.

---

29. The cases referred to are *Baxter v. Nicholson*, 363 N.C. 829 (2010), and *State v. Sullivan*, 201 N.C. App. 540 (2009), which are discussed in Trey Allen, *One Oath or Two? What is THE Oath of Office?* COATES' CANONS: NC LOC. GOV'T L. BLOG (Jan. 27, 2017), http://canons.sog.unc.edu/one-oath-or-two-what-is-the-oath-of-office.

30. G.S. 160A-62.

31. G.S. 11-7.1.

The deputy city clerk may administer the oath in place of the clerk, if the deputy is also a sworn officer.[32]

Pursuant to G.S. 160A-61, all oaths of office subscribed by elected or appointed city officers must be filed with the city clerk.

It is imperative that incoming council members refrain from undertaking their duties before they are sworn. Under G.S. 14-229, an individual who undertakes the duties of a public office without first taking, subscribing, and filing the oath of office is guilty of a Class 1 misdemeanor. Similarly, G.S. 128-5 provides that any person who enters upon the duties of a public office without first taking the oath of office shall be subject to a forfeiture of $500 (to be used for the poor of the county). Both statutes authorize an offender's ejectment from office.

(c) Selection of [Mayor and] Mayor Pro Tempore. As the second order of business at the organizational meeting, the council shall elect from among its members [a mayor and] a mayor pro tempore using the procedures specified in Rule 38. [The mayor shall serve for [a certain term] [at the pleasure of the council]]. The mayor pro tempore shall [likewise] serve at the council's pleasure.

> **Comment:** In most cities, the people elect the mayor directly. The bracketed reference in paragraph (c) to the mayor's election at the organizational meeting is appropriate only for a city with a charter that directs the council to choose the mayor from among its members. If the mayor is elected by the council, the charter may provide that he or she serves either for a fixed term or at the council's pleasure. ("[A]t the council's pleasure" means that the council may vote to replace the mayor at any regular meeting or any special meeting called for that purpose.)
>
> State law requires every city council to select a mayor pro tempore at its organizational meeting.[33] See Rule 18 for the duties of the mayor pro tempore, which include presiding over council meetings in the mayor's absence. Unless the charter provides otherwise, the mayor pro tempore serves at the council's pleasure.

---

32. G.S. 11-8.
33. G.S. 160A-70.

Part V. Types of Meetings

Rule 9. Regular Meetings

(a) Regular Meeting Schedule. The council shall hold a regular meeting on the [first and third] [Monday] of each month, except that if a regular meeting day is a legal holiday, the meeting shall be held on the next business day. The meeting shall be held at [_____] and begin at [_____]. The council shall adopt a meeting schedule each year consistent with this rule. A copy of the council's current meeting schedule shall be filed with the city clerk [and posted on the city's website].

> **Comment:** Pursuant to G.S. 160A-71, the council must fix the time and place for regular meetings. If it does not do so, the council must hold a regular meeting at 10 a.m. on the first Monday of each month.[34] A council that adopts a regular meeting schedule may choose to meet less frequently than once per month, unless its charter mandates monthly meetings. The open meetings law requires the council's schedule of regular meetings to be kept on file with the city clerk.[35] The law further directs that the council post the schedule on its website, if it has one.[36]

(b) Change to Meeting Schedule. Notwithstanding paragraph (a) of this rule, the council may amend its regular meeting schedule to add or delete meetings or to change the date, time, or location of one or more meetings on the schedule. The amended schedule shall be filed with the city clerk at least seven (7) calendar days before the day of the first meeting held pursuant to the revised schedule [and posted on the city's website].

> **Comment:** The seven-day filing requirement is imposed by the open meetings law.[37] If the council has a website, the open meetings law obliges the council to post the amended schedule there.[38]

Rule 10. Special Meetings

(a) Calling Special Meetings. A special meeting of the council may be called by the mayor, the mayor pro tempore, or any two council members. A

---

34. G.S. 160A-71(a).
35. G.S. 143-318.12(a).
36. G.S. 143-318.12(d).
37. G.S. 143-318.12(a).
38. G.S. 143-318.12(d).

special meeting may also be called by vote of the council in open session during a regular meeting or another duly called special meeting.

> **Comment:** The two methods of calling a special meeting set out above are authorized in G.S. 160A-71(b)(1). The same statutory provision also permits the members of a council to conduct a special meeting anytime all of them are gathered in the same place or any member not present has signed a written waiver of notice. This third method is not included in this rule because a council that made use of it would violate the open meetings law's requirement—reflected in paragraph (b) of this rule—to provide the public with a minimum of forty-eight hours' notice of each special meeting.

(b) Notice to the Public. At least forty-eight hours before a special meeting of the council, notice of the date, time, place, and purpose of the meeting shall be (1) posted on the council's principal bulletin board or, if the council has no such board, at the door of the council's usual meeting room and (2) delivered, e-mailed, or mailed to each newspaper, wire service, radio station, television station, and person who has filed a written request for notice with the city clerk. Furthermore, if the council has a website maintained by at least one city employee, notice of the special meeting's date, time, place, and purpose shall be posted on the website in advance of the meeting.

> **Comment:** This subsection incorporates the open meetings law's public notice requirements for special meetings.[39]

(c) Notice to Members.

(1) *Meeting called by the mayor, the mayor pro tempore, or any two council members.* At least forty-eight hours before a special meeting called by the mayor, the mayor pro tempore, or any two council members, written notice of the meeting stating its date, time, and place, as well as the subjects to be considered, shall be delivered to the mayor and each council member or left at his or her usual dwelling place.

(2) *Meeting called by vote of the council in open session.* When a special meeting is called by vote of the council in open session during a regular meeting or another duly called special meeting, the motion or resolution calling the special meeting shall state the meeting's date, time, place, and purpose. [Written notice of the special meeting's date, time, place, and purpose shall be mailed or delivered at least forty-

---

39. G.S. 143-318.12(b)(2), (e).

eight hours before the meeting to each council member not present for the meeting at which the special meeting was called, and to the mayor if he or she was not present at that meeting.]

Comment: The notice to individual council members required under subparagraph (c)(1) of this rule tracks G.S. 160A-71(b)(1), except that the statutory provision mandates only six hours' notice. Subparagraph (c)(1) increases that notice to forty-eight hours on the assumption that members want to be notified of special meetings at least as far ahead of time as the public.

Although G.S. 160A-71(b)(1) does not mandate that individual members receive notice of a special meeting called in accordance with subparagraph (c)(2), the suggested language in brackets requires such notification in order to ensure that members who are not present when a special meeting is called receive word of the meeting.

(d) Transacting Other Business. Unless all members are present or any absent member has signed a written waiver of notice, only those items of business specified in the notice to council members may be taken up at a special meeting. [Even when all members are present or any absent member has signed a waiver, the council may take up an item of business not covered by the notice only if the council first determines in good faith that the item must be discussed or acted upon immediately.]

Comment: Under G.S. 160A-71(b)(1), a special meeting called by the mayor, mayor pro tempore, or any two council members may address matters not listed in the notice provided to members, but only if all members are in attendance or any absent member has signed a written waiver of notice. Paragraph (d) of this rule extends that same limitation to any special meeting called by a vote of the council in a regular or another duly called special meeting.

The bracketed optional sentence in paragraph (d) places a further restriction on the council's ability to turn to matters at a special meeting that were not listed on the notice to members. Specifically, the bracketed sentence declares that the council may not take up such a matter unless it first concludes in good faith that the item must be discussed or acted upon immediately. This restriction is intended to reduce the likelihood of a violation of the open meetings law, which, as noted in the *Comment* to paragraph (b), requires the public notice of a special meeting to articulate the meeting's purpose. While nothing in the open meetings law expressly prohibits the council from taking up an unannounced matter at a special meeting if the requirements of G.S. 160A-71(b)(1) are met, the bracketed sentence in paragraph (d) assumes that the council should avoid doing so when the matter is not urgent.[40]

Rule 11. Emergency Meetings

(a) Grounds for Emergency Meeting. Emergency meetings of the city council may be called only to address generally unexpected circumstances demanding the council's immediate attention.

(b) Calling Emergency Meetings. There are two methods by which an emergency meeting of the council may be called.

(1) The mayor, the mayor pro tempore, or any two members of the council may at any time call an emergency council meeting by signing a written notice stating the date, time, and place of the meeting and the subjects to be considered. The notice shall be delivered to the mayor and each council member or left at his or her usual dwelling place at least six hours before the meeting.

(2) An emergency meeting may be held when the mayor and all members of the council are present and consent thereto, or when any absent member has signed a written waiver of notice.

(c) Notice to Media of Emergency Meetings. Notice of an emergency meeting shall be given to each local newspaper, local wire service, local radio station, and local television station that has filed a written request with the city clerk for notice of emergency meetings. To be valid, the request must include the newspaper's, wire service's, or station's telephone number. Notice may be given by telephone, e-mail, or the same method used to notify council members. Notice must be provided immediately after council members have been notified and at the expense of the party notified.

---

40. *See generally* Trey Allen, *Statutory Permission to Take Up Items Not on the Special Meeting Notice*, COATES' CANONS: NC LOC. GOV'T L. BLOG (Jan. 26, 2015), http://canons. sog.unc.edu/statutory-permission-to-take-up-items-not-on-the-special-meeting-notice/ (analyzing the impact of statutory notice provisions on the ability of a city council to consider matters at a special meeting that were not included on the meeting notice).

(d) Transaction of Other Business Prohibited. Only business connected with the emergency may be considered at an emergency meeting.

> **Comment:** Paragraphs (a), (c), and (d) of this rule state the requirements for emergency meetings under the open meetings law.[41] Since none of the provisions in the open meetings law or Chapter 160A specify the method for calling emergency meetings, paragraph (b) of this rule falls back on the procedures set out in G.S. 160A-71(b) for calling special meetings, with one exception. Under G.S. 160A-71(b)(3), a special meeting may be called by the council at any regular or duly called special meeting. Paragraph (b) omits that method because, if an emergency were to arise during a regular meeting, the council could amend its agenda to deal with it and the odds of an emergency arising during a special meeting are exceedingly small.

Rule 12. Recessed Meetings

(a) Calling Recessed Meetings. When conducting a properly called regular, special, or emergency meeting, the council may recess the meeting to another date, time, or place by a procedural motion made and adopted, as provided in Rule 31, Motion 3, in open session. The motion must state the time (including the date, if the meeting will resume on a different day) and place at which the meeting will reconvene.

(b) Notice of Recessed Meetings. If the council has a website maintained by one or more city employees, notice of the recessed meeting's date, time, and place must appear on the webpage prior to the meeting. No further notice of a properly called recessed meeting is required.

> **Comment:** This rule follows the open meetings law's requirements for recessed meetings.[42] The procedural mechanism for setting a recessed meeting is a motion to recess to a time and place certain (Rule 31, Motion 3). The motion must be made in open session, since under the open meetings law the adoption of such a motion is not listed as an action that is allowed during a closed session.[43]

---

41. G.S. 143-318.12(b)(3).
42. G.S. 143-318.12(b)(1), (e).
43. *See* G.S. 143-318.11 (listing the grounds on which a public body may enter closed session).

Part VI. Agenda

Rule 13. Agenda

(a) Draft Agenda.

(1) *Preparation.* The [city manager/administrator] [city clerk] shall prepare a draft agenda in advance of each meeting of the city council.

(2) *Requesting placement of items on draft agenda.* For a regular meeting, a request to have an item of business placed on the draft agenda must be received by the [city manager/administrator] [city clerk] at least [two] working days before the date of the meeting. The [city manager/administrator] [city clerk] must place an item on the draft agenda in response to a council member's timely request.

(3) *Supplemental information/materials.* If the council is expected to consider a proposed ordinance or ordinance amendment, a copy of the proposed ordinance or amendment shall be attached to the draft agenda. [An agenda package shall be prepared that includes, for each item of business listed on the draft agenda, as much background information on the topic as is available and feasible to provide.]

(4) *Delivery to council members.* Each council member shall receive a hard or electronic copy of the draft agenda [and the agenda package]. [Except in the case of an emergency meeting, the agenda [and agenda package] shall be furnished to each member at least [twenty-four hours] before the meeting.]

(5) *Public inspection.* The draft agenda [and agenda package] shall be available to the public when the document[s] [is/are] ready to be, or [has/have] been, circulated.

Comment: No statute requires a city council to use an agenda. Because of the volume and complexity of the matters they confront, many councils use agendas for most or all of their meetings anyway.

This rule describes a typical agenda preparation process. In some cities, the mayor plays a major role in preparing draft agendas. The council in such a city may wish to add language to subparagraph (a)(1) formalizing the mayor's place in agenda preparation.

Most councils that use agendas do so for any of three reasons.

- The first is to organize the materials that the council plans to consider. A council that makes use of agendas primarily for this reason is usually willing to allow last-minute additions to the agenda, if they are supported by a majority of members present and voting. That is the approach followed by this rule.

- The second reason that councils use agendas is to control the length of their meetings. A council that prefers to control meeting length will often hold an "agenda meeting" or a "work session" before its regular meeting so that members may ask questions and thoroughly explore proposals to be acted upon at their regular "business" meeting. A council that takes this approach may not wish to allow any late additions to the agenda unless an unexpected and pressing matter arises.

  ○ Regardless of what it is called, an agenda meeting or work session constitutes either a regular meeting or a special meeting for purposes of the open meetings law and G.S. 160A-71. It is a regular meeting if it appears on the council's duly adopted regular meeting schedule on file with the city clerk; otherwise, it is a special meeting. Consequently, agenda meetings and work sessions are subject to the notice and other pertinent requirements imposed by the open meetings law, G.S. 160A-71, and these rules.

- A third reason that city councils use agendas is to enable members to study matters prior to the meetings at which they will be considered. With this rationale in mind, subparagraph (a)(4) contains suggested wording that a council may adopt if it wants to direct that members have access to relevant documents in advance of non-emergency meetings. Some councils may want to employ a more targeted approach by describing the sorts of proposed orders, policies, regulations, resolutions, reports, or other records members should receive along with the draft agenda. Because ordinances can impose restrictions or obligations on individuals citywide, subparagraph (a)(3) mandates that any proposed ordinance or ordinance amendment be attached to the draft agenda so that members will have a clear understanding of what they are being asked to approve.

The city clerk or chief administrative officer may find it convenient to maintain a mailing list of interested parties who wish to receive copies of draft agendas and/or agenda packages. Inasmuch as the background materials attached to the draft agenda can be quite voluminous, the council may wish to charge those receiving the full agenda package for the cost of reproduction.

There is some uncertainty in the law over the point at which a draft agenda and any accompanying agenda package must be made available for inspection or copying in response to a public records request. The case law in North Carolina does not provide a clear answer to this question, but the safe approach seems to be to regard a draft agenda and agenda package as public records as soon as they are ready for circulation.[44] Their status as public records does not mandate that the city advertise their existence or post them online, however, merely that they be made available in response to public records requests. Of course, redaction may be necessary or permissible to the extent that the agenda package contains confidential, privileged, or non-public records.

(b) Adoption of the Agenda.

(1) *Adoption.* As its first order of business at each meeting, the council shall review the draft agenda, make whatever revisions it deems appropriate, and adopt a formal agenda for the meeting.

(2) *Amending the agenda.* Both before and after it adopts the agenda, the council may add or subtract agenda items by majority vote of the members present and voting, except that
- the council may not add to the items stated in the notice of a special meeting unless the requirements in Rule 10(d) are satisfied and
- only business connected with the emergency may be considered at an emergency meeting.

(3) *Designation of items "For Discussion and Possible Action."* The council may designate an agenda item "for discussion and possible action." The designation signifies that the council intends to discuss the item and may, if it so chooses, take action on the item following the discussion.

Comment: Although the council enjoys broad discretion in deciding what business it will conduct at a regular meeting, procedural

---

44. *See* Lawrence, *supra* note 25, at 15 ("[A] court might exclude . . . a draft [that is still in a very preliminary form] from the definition of public record, at least until the authority begins to circulate it to others, but there appears to be little other room for excluding from public access documents that are closer to completion.").

requirements imposed by state law on certain undertakings prevent the council from taking some actions without warning. For instance, the council may not amend the text of a zoning ordinance, even at a regular meeting, unless the published notice and public hearing mandated by G.S. 160A-364 have been provided.[45]

As explained in the *Comment* to Rule 10(d), a city council stands on shaky legal ground when it adds to the agenda of a special meeting agenda items that did not appear in the public notice of the meeting required by the open meetings law. Subparagraph (b)(2) of this rule therefore prohibits adding items to the agenda for a special meeting, except in compliance with Rule 10(d). Likewise, in accordance with G.S. 143-318.12(b)(3), the agenda for an emergency meeting is confined by subparagraph (b)(2) to business connected with the emergency.

It is commonplace for council members to want to discuss an issue informally, even when they are unsure about whether they will ultimately take action on the matter. Under subparagraph (b)(3), by designating particular agenda items "for discussion and possible action," the council preserves the option of taking action if discussion leads to agreement on a course of action.

(c) Consent Agenda. The council may designate part of an agenda for a regular meeting as the *consent agenda*. Items may be placed on the consent agenda by the person(s) charged with preparing the draft agenda if the items are judged to be noncontroversial and routine. Prior to the council's adoption of the meeting agenda under subparagraph (b)(1) of this rule, the request of any member to have an item moved from the consent agenda to unfinished business must be honored by the council. All items on the consent agenda must be voted on and adopted by a single motion, with the minutes reflecting the motion and vote for each item.

> **Comment:** The consent agenda groups together items that the individuals who prepare the draft agenda regard as noncontroversial and routine. This procedural tool can improve efficiency by enabling the council to dispose of multiple matters with a single motion and vote.

---

45. Notice of the public hearing on the proposed adoption, amendment, or repeal of a zoning ordinance must be published twice in a newspaper of general circulation, once a week for two successive calendar weeks, with publication of the first notice occurring not fewer than 10 days and not more than 25 days before the hearing date. G.S. 160A-364(a).

The council reviews the consent agenda during its examination of the draft agenda at the outset of a meeting. Each member is free to ask for the removal of one or more items from the consent agenda. Such a request must be honored, and the item(s) in question must be treated as unfinished business. The council may then approve the remaining items on the consent agenda simultaneously through the adoption of a single motion. As a matter of law, the council's action constitutes a motion and vote on each item, and in keeping with this understanding, the minutes should record a separate motion and vote for each item approved as part of the consent agenda.

Because the consent agenda is voted on at the outset of a meeting, items likely to generate significant public interest should not be placed on the consent agenda, especially when the meeting includes a public comment period. If the council uses the consent agenda to dispose of controversial as well as routine matters before the public comment period, members of the public may conclude that the council does not value their input.

Moreover, the consent agenda should not mix items with different voting requirements. If the minimum number of affirmative votes necessary for adoption is not the same for all items on the consent agenda, the council could create a situation in which some but not all of the consent agenda has been approved. A motion to approve the minutes of a prior meeting, for example, passes so long as it receives more than half of the votes cast, a quorum being present. On the other hand, as explained in more detail in the *Comment* to Rule 33, an affirmative vote by two-thirds of the council is usually necessary to approve a proposed ordinance on the date of introduction.

(d) Informal Discussion of Agenda Items. The council may informally discuss an agenda item even when no motion regarding that item is pending.

> **Comment:** Standard parliamentary practice does not permit debate on a matter in the absence of a pending motion.[46] Small boards, though, can often benefit from informal discussion prior to the making of any motion. Indeed, *Robert's Rules of Order* expressly allows small boards—defined as boards with twelve or fewer members—to engage in informal discussion of an issue while no

---

46. *RONR* (11th ed.) 34, ll. 7–9.

motion is pending.[47] Paragraph (d) of this rule follows *Robert's* on this point. If informal discussion results in a motion, debate on the motion should be conducted pursuant to Rule 25.

Rule 14. Acting by Reference to Agenda or Other Document

The council shall not deliberate, vote, or otherwise take action on any matter by reference to the agenda or any other document with the intention of preventing persons in attendance from understanding what action is being considered or undertaken. The council may deliberate and vote by reference to the agenda or any item on the agenda, including the consent agenda, provided copies of the agenda are available for public inspection at the meeting and are sufficiently worded to enable the public to understand what is being deliberated or acted upon.

> **Comment:** The open meetings law restricts the ability of public bodies to act by reference.[48] This rule complies with those restrictions.

Rule 15. Agenda Items from Members of the Public

If a member of the public wishes to request that the council include an item on its regular meeting agenda, he or she must submit the request to the [city clerk/city manager/administrator] by the deadline specified in Rule 13(a)(2). The council is not obligated to place an item on the agenda merely because such a request has been received.

> **Comment:** While it is not unusual for members of the public to ask that an item be placed on the council's meeting agenda, the council has no legal obligation to honor such requests. The open meetings law guarantees the public's right to attend council meetings, but control of the agenda belongs to the council. Yet a total refusal to consider agenda requests from residents and other interested persons could lead to negative perceptions of the council. This rule creates a mechanism for the submission of agenda requests while plainly stating that the council may choose not to act on them.

---

47. *RONR* (11th ed.) 488, ll. 7–8.
48. G.S. 143-318.13(c).

Rule 16. Order of Business

Items shall be placed on a regular meeting agenda according to the order of business. The usual order of business for each regular meeting shall be as follows:

- adoption of the agenda,
- approval of the consent agenda,
- approval of the previous meeting minutes,
- public hearings,
- public comments,
- administrative reports,
- committee reports,
- unfinished business, and
- new business.

Without objection, the mayor may call agenda items in any order most convenient for the dispatch of business.

> **Comment:** This rule's placement of public hearings and the public comment period ahead of reports and unfinished and new business benefits members of the public in two ways: (1) they may address the council without having to stay for the whole meeting, and (2) they have the chance to comment on items of new or unfinished business prior to action by the council. Likewise, by putting reports before old and new business, the suggested order of business may afford at least some staff and committee members the option of leaving prior to adjournment.
>
> For purposes of these rules, unfinished business consists of matters carried over from a previous meeting, either because the council adjourned without completing its order of business or because it adopted a motion postponing the matters until the present meeting.[49]

---

49. *See* Rule 31, Motion 10 (Motion to Postpone to a Certain Time).

Part VII. Role of the Presiding Officer

Rule 17. The Mayor

(a) Presiding Officer. When present, the mayor shall preside at meetings of the council.

> **Comment:** Although state law invests the mayor with few formal powers, it expressly provides that the mayor is to preside at all council meetings.[50]

(b) Right to Vote. The mayor [may vote only when an equal number of affirmative and negative votes have been cast] [votes on the same basis as other council members, though in no event may the mayor break a tie on a motion on which he or she has already voted].

> **Comment:** Under G.S. 160A-69, the mayor has the right to vote only when there are an equal number of affirmative and negative votes, unless the mayor is elected by the council from among its membership and the city charter is silent on the matter. In that case the mayor has the right to vote on all matters but not to break a tie on a motion on which he or she has already voted. Many cities have charter provisions dealing with the mayor's voting rights; such provisions take precedence over G.S. 160A-69 and this rule.

(c) Recognition of Members. A member must be recognized by the mayor (or other presiding officer) in order to address the council, but recognition is not necessary for an appeal pursuant to Rule 31, Motion 1.

> **Comment:** Standard parliamentary practice does not permit a member to address a body until he or she has first been recognized by the presiding officer.[51] On the other hand, the presiding officer must recognize any member who seeks the floor and is entitled to it.[52] Additionally, under Rule 31, Motion 1, if a member's purpose in seeking the floor is to appeal a procedural ruling by the mayor, the member may make the appeal regardless of whether the mayor

---

50. G.S. 160A-69. *See also* Vaughn M. Upshaw, *County and City Governing Boards, in* County and Municipal Government in North Carolina 31 (Frayda S. Bluestein ed., 2d ed. 2014) (summarizing the mayor's powers); Frayda S. Bluestein, *Powers of Mayors,* Coates' Canons: NC Loc. Gov't L. Blog (Dec. 23, 2009), http://canons.sog.unc.edu/powers-of-mayors (same).

51. *RONR* (11th ed.) 376, ll. 13–16.

52. *RONR* (11th ed.) 376, l. 16; 377, l. 1.

recognizes him or her. If recognition by the mayor were necessary in that situation, the mayor could defeat the appeal simply by refusing to call on the member.

(d) Powers as Presiding Officer. As presiding officer, the mayor is to enforce these rules and maintain order and decorum during council meetings. To that end, the mayor may

(1) rule on points of parliamentary procedure, to include ruling out of order any motion clearly offered for obstructive or dilatory purposes;
(2) determine whether a member or other speaker has gone beyond reasonable standards of courtesy in his or her remarks and entertain and rule on objections from other members on this ground;
(3) entertain and answer questions of parliamentary procedure;
(4) call a brief recess at any time; and
(5) adjourn in an emergency.

> **Comment:** The term "recess" is defined in *Robert's Rules of Order* as "a short intermission in the assembly's proceedings, commonly of only a few minutes, which does not close the meeting and after which business will immediately be resumed at exactly the point where it was interrupted."[53]
>
> Subparagraph (d)(4) of this rule allows the mayor to call for a brief recess in the belief that council members can sometimes benefit from a "cooling off" period, especially when contentious topics are under consideration.[54] Ideally, the mayor, in his or her capacity as presiding officer, will be well placed to ascertain when a short break might help ease tensions at a council meeting.
>
> Whether and when to adjourn is normally a decision for the council to make through a motion and vote, but subparagraph (d)(5) authorizes the mayor to adjourn a meeting of the council "in an emergency." The equivalent provision in *Robert's* offers some guidance regarding the type of event that would justify an emergency adjournment by the mayor: "In the event of a fire, riot, or other extreme emergency, if the

---

53. *RONR* (11th ed.) 230, ll. 20–23.

54. The mayor's unilateral authority to call for a brief recess goes beyond the powers of presiding officers under *Robert's Rules of Order*. According to *Robert's*, a recess may be taken only on a motion and vote by the members, except when a recess is provided for in the meeting agenda. *RONR* (11th ed.) § 20, at 230–33.

chair believes taking time for a vote on adjourning would be dangerous to those present, he should declare the meeting adjourned. . . ."[55]

(e) Appeals of Procedural Rulings. A member may appeal a decision made or answer given by the mayor under subparagraph (d)(1), (2), or (3) in accordance with Rule 31, Motion 1.

Rule 18. The Mayor Pro Tempore

(a) Presiding in Mayor's Absence. When present, the mayor pro tempore shall preside over council meetings in the mayor's absence with all the powers specified in Rule 17(d).

(b) Delegation of Mayor's Powers/Duties. In the mayor's absence, the council may confer on the mayor pro tempore any of the mayor's powers and duties. Likewise, if the mayor becomes physically or mentally unable to perform the duties of his or her office, the council may by unanimous vote declare the mayor incapacitated and confer any of the mayor's powers and duties on the mayor pro tempore. When the mayor announces that he or she is no longer incapacitated, and a majority of the council concurs, the mayor shall resume the exercise of his or her powers and duties.

(c) Duty to Vote. Even when presiding over a council meeting, the mayor pro tempore has the same duty as other members to vote on all questions unless he or she has been excused from voting on a matter in accordance with Rule 28.

> **Comment:** This rule largely paraphrases G.S. 160A-70. It also clarifies that the duty to vote imposed on council members by G.S. 160A-75 continues to apply to the mayor pro tempore when he or she presides over a council meeting in the mayor's absence.

Rule 19. Other Presiding Officer

If both the mayor and mayor pro tempore are absent, the council may elect from among its members a temporary presiding officer to chair the meeting. While serving as temporary presiding officer, a member has the powers listed in Rule 17(d). Service as a temporary presiding officer does not relieve

---

55. *RONR* (11th ed.) 86, ll. 26–29.

a member of the duty to vote on all questions unless excused from voting pursuant to Rule 28.

> **Comment:** General Statute 160A-70 expressly authorizes a city council to select one of its members to preside over a council meeting when neither the mayor nor the mayor pro tempore is there.

Rule 20. When the Presiding Officer Is Active in Debate

If the mayor becomes active in debate on a particular proposal, he or she [may] [must] have the mayor pro tempore preside during the council's consideration of the matter. If the mayor pro tempore is absent or is also actively debating the matter, the mayor [may] [must] designate another member to preside until the matter is concluded. Similarly, if the mayor pro tempore or a temporary presiding officer is presiding and takes an active part in debating a topic, he or she [may] [must] designate another council member to preside temporarily.

> **Comment:** When it comes to presiding officers, good leadership depends, to a certain degree, on not taking sides during a debate. If the presiding officer does take a position in debate, members on the other side of an issue might suspect that any procedural rulings detrimental to their cause result more from the presiding officer's desire to promote a certain outcome than from the impartial application of parliamentary principles. Yet on a small board, especially one composed of elected officials chosen to represent the people, it may not always be feasible or even desirable for the presiding officer to withhold his or her views. By providing that the gavel may or must be temporarily relinquished, this rule makes it possible for the mayor or other presiding officer to participate in a debate without unduly compromising his or her reputation for even-handedness.

Part VIII. Motions and Voting

Rule 21. Action by the Council

Except as otherwise provided in these rules, the council shall act by motion. Any member may make a motion, [not] including the mayor.

> **Comment:** The mayor's voting status should determine whether the mayor is allowed to offer motions at council meetings. In a city with a

mayor who may vote only to break a tie, the mayor should not make motions because he or she has no say in whether a motion passes except when the members who vote are evenly divided. (The mayor may invite a desired motion, however, by saying, "The Chair will entertain a motion that . . . ," or words to that effect.)

In a city where the mayor votes on the same basis as council members, he or she should enjoy the same right to offer motions as any member of the council. Nonetheless, the mayor could reasonably decide to refrain from making motions in the belief that, as presiding officer, he or she ought to avoid expressing his or her views during debate on a proposed action.

There are a few situations in which these rules empower the council to act by procedural mechanisms other than a motion and vote. Rule 27 provides that a member's request to change his or her vote may be granted by unanimous consent in certain situations. Rule 29 permits the council to determine by unanimous consent that it will vote on a pending motion by written ballot. Finally, Rule 38 directs the council to act by nomination rather than by motion when filling vacancies on the council or appointed bodies.

Rule 22. Second Not Required

No second is required on any motion.

Comment: It is standard parliamentary practice to refuse to entertain any motion that does not receive a second. The purpose of requiring a second "is to prevent time from being consumed by the assembly's having to dispose of a motion that only one person wants to see introduced."[56] This rationale makes sense as applied to large bodies. It would be grossly inefficient, for example, for a 100-member body to debate a motion that not one of its members is willing to second. On the other hand, this reasoning is not persuasive as to small boards, where even a single member constitutes a significant percentage of a board's total membership. On a five-member board, for instance, a motion presumably starts with the backing of 20 percent of the members. The limited utility of seconds in the case

---

56. *RONR* (11th ed.) 36, ll. 28–31.

of small boards is acknowledged by *Robert's Rules of Order*, which recommends that small boards not require seconds for motions.[57]

When it comes to the city council, the representative function of members also militates against requiring a second. Arguably, because each council member speaks not just for himself or herself but for the member's constituents as well, a motion warrants the council's attention, regardless of whether another member is willing to second it.

Rule 23. One Motion at a Time

A member may make only one motion at a time.

> **Comment:** "The purpose of meeting procedures is to allow members to reach informed . . . decisions in an effective, efficient, orderly, courteous, and fair manner."[58] Permitting members to make more than one motion at a time would undermine that purpose by creating enormous potential for confusion.

Rule 24. Withdrawal of Motion

The member who introduces a motion may withdraw the motion unless the motion has been amended or the presiding officer has put the motion to a vote.

> **Comment:** Under *Robert's Rules of Order*, the member who makes a motion may withdraw it without anyone's consent until the presiding officer states the motion.[59] Once the motion has been stated by the presiding officer, ownership of the motion transfers to the body, and the member may not withdraw it without the body's consent.[60] Inasmuch as the *Robert's* approach seems unduly restrictive for small boards, this rule permits a council member who has made a motion to withdraw it unless the council has made the motion its own by amending it or the presiding officer has called for a vote on the motion.

---

57. *RONR* (11th ed.) 488, l. 1.
58. Standard Code 2.
59. *RONR* (11th ed.) 295, ll. 31–33.
60. *RONR* (11th ed.) 296, ll. 21–25.

Rule 25. Debate

The presiding officer shall state the motion and then open the floor to debate, presiding over the debate according to the principles listed below.

- The maker of the motion is entitled to speak first.
- A member who has not spoken on the issue shall be recognized before a member who has already spoken.
- To the extent practicable, the debate shall alternate between proponents and opponents of the measure.
- [No member may speak more than twice on the same substantive motion. A member's first speech on a substantive motion shall be limited to [10] minutes, and any second speech on the same motion shall be limited to [five] minutes. The same rules apply to debate on a procedural motion, except that a member's first speech shall not exceed [five] minutes, and any second speech shall be limited to [two] minutes.]

> **Comment:** The first three principles set out in this rule follow guidelines for debate found in *Robert's Rules of Order*.[61] The suggested language in brackets at the end of this rule is similar to Rule 10(b) in the procedural rules for the North Carolina House of Representatives. Not all councils will find it desirable to include the suggested language, and any council that decides to include it should carefully evaluate whether its proposed time limits suit the council's particular situation.

Rule 26. Adoption by Majority Vote

A motion is adopted if supported by a simple majority of the votes cast, a quorum being present, except when a larger majority is required by these rules or state law.

> **Comment:** Consistent with general parliamentary practice, this rule provides that a motion passes in most instances if supported by more than half of the votes cast, so long as a quorum is present.[62]

---

61. *RONR* (11th ed.) 379, ll. 10–13, 27–35; 380, ll. 1–2.

62. "[T]he basic requirement for approval of an action or choice by a deliberative assembly, except where a rule provides otherwise, is a *majority vote*. The word *majority* means 'more than half'; and when the term *majority vote* is used without qualification . . . it means more than half of the votes cast by persons entitled to vote, excluding blanks or abstentions, at a regular or properly called meeting." *RONR* (11th ed.) 400, ll. 5–12 (emphases in original).

Yet some actions require more than a simple majority of votes cast. For example, as reflected in Rule 33, state law prohibits the council from adopting an ordinance on the same day that it is introduced unless the votes cast in support of the ordinance equal or exceed two-thirds of the council's actual membership, excluding vacant seats and counting the mayor only if the mayor may vote on all questions.[63] Furthermore, a supermajority is needed to adopt some of the procedural motions listed in Rule 31.

Not every statutory supermajority requirement is represented in these rules. The council should consult its attorney about whether a proposed action triggers such a requirement.

Rule 27. Changing a Vote

A member may change his or her vote on a motion at any time before the presiding officer announces whether the motion has passed or failed. Once the presiding officer announces the result, a member may not change his or her vote without the unanimous consent of the remaining members present. A member's request for unanimous consent to change a vote is not in order unless made immediately following the presiding officer's announcement of the result.

> **Comment:** This rule largely adopts but also simplifies the approach taken by *Robert's Rules of Order* to vote changes.[64]
>
> Members need not actually cast votes to grant a colleague's request for unanimous consent to change a vote. The presiding officer may simply ask whether there is any objection and, hearing none, pronounce the request approved.[65]

Rule 28. Duty to Vote

(a) Duty to Vote. Every council member must vote except when excused from voting as provided by this rule.

---

63. G.S. 160A-75.

64. *See RONR* (11th ed.) 408, ll. 21–36; 409, ll. 1–10 (detailing the steps necessary for a vote change). *See also* Trey Allen, *When May a Board Member Change a Vote?* COATES' CANONS: NC LOC. GOV'T L. BLOG (June 15, 2015), http://canons.sog.unc.edu/when-may-a-board-member-change-a-vote (same).

65. *RONR* (11th ed.) 54, ll. 13–29.

(b) Grounds for Excusal. A member may be excused from voting on a matter involving the member's own financial interest or official conduct, though not if the proposal in question is one to alter the compensation or allowances paid to council members. Members may also be excused from voting when prohibited from voting under G.S. 14-234 (contract providing direct benefit to member), G.S. 160A-381(d) (legislative zoning decision likely to have a direct, substantial, and readily identifiable financial impact on member), or G.S. 160A-388(e)(2) (member's participation in quasi-judicial decision would violate affected person's right to an impartial decision maker). [Questions about whether a basis for excusal exists should be directed to the city attorney.]

(c) Procedure for Excusal.

(1) *At member's request.* Upon being recognized at a duly called meeting of the council, a member who wishes to be excused from voting shall so inform the presiding officer, who must then submit the matter to a vote of the remaining members present. If a majority of the remaining members present vote to excuse the member, the member is excused from voting on the matter.

(2) *On council's initiative.* Even when a member has not asked to be excused from voting on a matter, a majority of the remaining council members present may by motion and vote excuse the member from voting if grounds for doing so exist under paragraph (b).

(d) Consequence of Non-Excused Failure to Vote. Except as specified in paragraph (e), if a member who has not been excused from voting fails to vote on a matter, the member's failure to vote shall be recorded as an affirmative vote, provided

(1) the member is physically present in the council chamber or

(2) the member has physically withdrawn from the meeting without being excused by majority vote of the remaining members present.

(e) Failure to Vote on Certain Zoning Matters. A member's unexcused failure to vote shall not be recorded as an affirmative vote if the motion concerns a proposal to amend, supplement, or repeal a zoning ordinance. Instead, the member's unexcused failure to vote shall be recorded as an abstention.

> **Comment:** This rule essentially restates the voting rules set out in the first paragraph of G.S. 160A-75. It is not always easy to determine whether a basis for excusal exists, so the bracketed sentence at the

end of paragraph (b) advises the council to consult the city attorney when it is unsure about whether excusal is proper.[66]

State law does not describe the procedure for excusing a member from voting or even who, exactly, should do the excusing. Although in some cities the mayor rules on excusal requests, ultimate authority to grant or deny such requests plainly lies with the council.[67] Accordingly, paragraph (c) of this rule instructs the presiding officer to submit an excusal request to the council for a vote.

In 2015, the General Assembly amended G.S. 160A-75 to say that a member's unexcused failure to vote may not be recorded as an affirmative vote if the vote was taken under G.S. 160A-385, the statute authorizing city councils to amend, supplement, and repeal zoning ordinances.[68] For this reason, paragraph (e) of this rule declares that a member's unexcused failure to vote on such a matter must be recorded as an abstention.

[(f) Mayor's Duty to Vote. The provisions of this rule apply to the mayor.]

Comment: Paragraph (f) should be omitted unless the council elects the mayor from among its members. In that situation, the mayor has the same obligation to vote as any member, and his or her unexcused failure to vote must be treated like any member's unexcused failure to vote.[69] Except where the charter provides otherwise, a mayor who is elected directly by the people may vote only in the case of a tie, and even then the mayor may choose not to vote.[70]

---

66. For a helpful overview of the ethical conflicts that can justify excusal, see Frayda S. Bluestein & Norma R. Houston, *Ethics and Conflicts of Interest, in* County and Municipal Government in North Carolina 115–24 (Frayda S. Bluestein ed., 2d ed. 2014).

67. *Compare* G.S. 160A-12 ("A power, function, right, privilege, or immunity that is conferred or imposed by charter or the general law without directions or restrictions as to how it is to be exercised or performed shall be carried into execution as provided by ordinance or resolution of the city council.") *and* G.S. 160A-67 ("Except as otherwise provided by law, the government and general management of the city shall be vested in the council. The powers and duties of the mayor shall be such as are conferred upon him by law, together with such other powers and duties as may be conferred upon him by the council pursuant to law.").

68. S.L. 2015-160, § 5.

69. Frayda S. Bluestein, *Do Mayors Have a Duty to Vote?* Coates' Canons: NC Loc. Gov't L. Blog (Nov. 7, 2013), http://canons.sog.unc.edu/do-mayors-have-a-duty-to-vote.

70. *Id.* If the mayor refuses to break a tie, the effect is that the motion fails for lack of a majority. *See RONR* (11th ed.) 405, ll. 28–29 ("On a tie vote, a motion requiring a majority vote for adoption is lost, since a tie is not a majority.").

Rule 29. Voting by Written Ballot

(a) Secret Ballots Prohibited. The council may not vote by secret ballot.

(b) Rules for Written Ballots. The council may decide by majority vote or unanimous consent to vote on a motion by written ballot. Each member must sign his or her ballot, and the minutes must record how each member voted by name. The ballots must be made available for public inspection in the city clerk's office immediately following the meeting at which the vote took place and remain there until the minutes of that meeting are approved, at which time the ballots may be destroyed.

> **Comment:** This rule paraphrases the open meetings law's provisions on a public body's use of written ballots.[71] Although the council may decide by majority vote to cast written ballots on a motion, paragraph (b) also allows it to make such a determination by unanimous consent to avoid the awkwardness of members voting on how to vote. The steps for obtaining unanimous consent are described in the *Comment* to Rule 27.

Rule 30. Substantive Motions

A substantive motion is not in order if made while another motion is pending. Once the council disposes of a substantive motion, it may not take up a motion that presents essentially the same issue at the same meeting, unless it first adopts a motion to reconsider pursuant to Rule 31, Motion 14.

> **Comment:** A substantive motion is one that brings new business before the council, such as a motion to adopt an amendment to a zoning ordinance.[72] A substantive motion may propose any action within the council's legal authority. Moreover, because Rule 21 requires the council to proceed by motion in most situations, ordinarily a substantive motion is the only way the council may act.
>
> A foundational principle of parliamentary procedure is that only one substantive proposal may be considered at any one time.[73] This

---

71. G.S. 143-318.13(b).

72. *RONR* (11th ed.) 100, ll. 3–4 ("[A] *main motion* is a motion whose introduction brings business before the assembly."). There is no mention in *Robert's Rules of Order* of substantive motions as such; the equivalent term in *Robert's* is main motion. *See generally RONR* (11th ed.) § 10 (describing characteristics of a main motion).

73. *See RONR* (11th ed.) 100, ll. 4–5 (noting that a main motion "can be made only when no other motion is pending").

rule therefore prohibits the introduction of a substantive motion while another motion is pending.

To promote efficiency, and consistent with *Robert's*, this rule also generally prevents a council from revisiting the subject matter of a substantive motion during the same meeting at which the motion was adopted or defeated.[74] The exception is when the council adopts a motion to reconsider the substantive motion, as provided in Rule 31, Motion 14.

Rule 31. Procedural Motions

(a) Certain Motions Allowed. The council may consider only those procedural motions listed in this rule. Unless otherwise noted, each procedural motion may be debated and amended and requires a majority of votes cast, a quorum being present, for adoption.

> **Comment:** For purposes of these rules, a procedural motion is any non-substantive motion. In most instances, a procedural motion, if adopted, acts on a substantive motion in some way, such as a motion to postpone the council's consideration of a substantive motion to another meeting.
>
> The array of motions in *Robert's Rules of Order* that would qualify as procedural motions under these rules could prove bewildering. This rule retains only those procedural motions that seem likely to aid the council in its conduct of business, and many of them have been modified to make them more user-friendly.
>
> Several of the procedural motions in *Robert's* are not subject to debate, which makes sense in that *Robert's* was written primarily with large assemblies in mind.[75] Valid concerns about efficiency can justify a large assembly's decision not to afford every member the right to speak on any and all motions. These rules favor debate on all motions, however, for three reasons: (1) the city council's small size makes extended debate on most procedural motions unlikely; (2) each council member should be heard in debate because members represent not only themselves but also their constituents; and

---

74. *See RONR* (11th ed.) 111, ll. 11–15 (observing that typically "[n]o main motion is in order that presents substantially the same question as a motion that was finally disposed of earlier in the same session").

75. Under *Robert's*, for example, a motion to suspend the rules is not debatable. *RONR* (11th ed.) 261, l. 12.

(3) procedural mechanisms such as Motion 9 below can bring debate to a close if it becomes too time-consuming.

(b) Priority of Motions. The procedural motions set out in this paragraph are listed in order of priority. A procedural motion is not in order so long as another procedural motion of higher priority is pending, except that

- any procedural motion other than an appeal under Motion 1 is subject to amendment as provided in Motion 12, and
- a motion to call the question (end debate) may be made with regard to any procedural motion in accordance with Motion 9.

When several procedural motions are pending, voting must begin with the procedural motion highest in priority, provided that a motion to amend or end debate on the highest priority motion must be voted on first.

> **Comment:** As in *Robert's*, here the order of priority establishes which procedural motion yields to which—that is, which procedural motions may be made and considered while another one is pending.[76]
>
> The procedural motions described in this rule are summarized in table form in Appendix B.

Motion 1. To Appeal a Ruling of the Presiding Officer. Any member may appeal the presiding officer's ruling on whether a motion is in order or on whether a speaker has violated reasonable standards of courtesy. The presiding officer's response to a question of parliamentary procedure may also be appealed by any member. An appeal is in order immediately after the disputed ruling or parliamentary response and at no other time. The member who moves to appeal need not be recognized by the presiding officer, and if timely made, the motion may not be ruled out of order.

> **Comment:** Rule 17(e) recognizes that members may appeal the presiding officer's rulings on most procedural matters and answers to questions of parliamentary procedure. Motion 1 is the vehicle for such an appeal. It is accorded the highest priority among procedural motions, in part because it is untimely if not made immediately. Another reason for ranking it first among procedural motions is to ensure that rulings on all other procedural motions are subject to appeal.

---

76. *See generally RONR* (11th ed.) 61, ll. 11–35; 62, ll. 1–10 (explaining *RONR*'s basic approach to ranking motions).

Motion 2. To Adjourn. This motion may be used to close a meeting. It is not in order if the council is in closed session.

> **Comment:** Unlike the motion to adjourn described in Robert's, this motion is debatable and amendable.[77] Like the *Robert's* motion to adjourn, this motion may interrupt deliberation on a pending matter.[78] Why should the council be allowed to adjourn when business is pending? Because a vote to adjourn in such circumstances would signal that the council was not prepared to take action on one or more pending matters, and these rules disfavor forcing the council to act before it is ready.

Motion 3. To Recess to a Time and Place Certain. This motion may be used to call a recessed meeting as permitted under Rule 12. The motion must state the time (including the date, if the meeting will reconvene on a different day) and place at which the meeting will resume. The motion is not in order if the council is in closed session.

> **Comment:** This motion is analogous to the motion to fix the time for an adjourned meeting in *Robert's*, though, unlike that motion, this motion is debatable.[79] In deference to the open meetings law, which allows a public body to "recess[] a regular, special, or emergency meeting" to another "time and place," these rules employ the term "recessed meeting" instead of "adjourned meeting."[80]

Motion 4. To Take a Brief Recess.

> **Comment:** This motion allows the council to pause a meeting for a few minutes. It should not be confused with a motion to recess to a time and place certain under Motion 3. In contrast to *Robert's*, these rules allow debate on a motion to take a brief recess.[81] If debate on the motion becomes prolonged, the mayor may render both the motion

---

77. *RONR* (11th ed.) 236, ll. 7–8.

78. *RONR* (11th ed.) 233, ll. 17–33.

79. *See generally RONR* (11th ed.) § 22 at 242–46 (outlining the chief characteristics of a motion to fix the time to which to adjourn).

80. G.S. 143-318.12(b)(1). The terms "recessed" and "adjourned" are treated as synonymous in G.S. 160A-71(b1) ("Any regular or duly called special meeting may be recessed to reconvene at a time and place certain, or may be adjourned to reconvene at a time and place certain, by the council.").

81. *RONR* (11th ed.) 231, l. 30.

and the debate superfluous by unilaterally recessing the meeting for a short time pursuant to Rule 17(d)(4).

Motion 5. To Follow the Agenda. This motion must be made at the time an item of business that deviates from the agenda is proposed; otherwise, the motion is out of order as to that item.

> **Comment:** This motion is loosely patterned on the call for the orders of the day in *Robert's*, though unlike a call for the orders of the day, a motion to follow the agenda is debatable.[82] If adopted, it curtails the mayor's freedom under Rule 16 to call agenda items out of order. If the council as a whole does not object to the deviation from the agenda, it may simply vote down the motion. Alternatively, the council may pass the motion but then amend the agenda in accordance with Rule 13(b)(2).

Motion 6. To Suspend the Rules. To be adopted, a motion to suspend the rules must receive affirmative votes equal to at least two-thirds of the council's actual membership, excluding vacant seats and not counting the mayor if the mayor votes only in case of a tie. The council may not suspend provisions in these rules that are required under state law.

> **Comment:** This motion is generally the same as the motion to suspend the rules in *Robert's*, except that it is debatable and amendable.[83] This motion is in order when the council wishes to take some action within its legal authority but one or more of these rules prevents it from doing so. For example, the council could use this motion in the middle of regular meeting to permit consideration of a proposed noise ordinance that is not on the agenda. (Of course, the council could reach the same result by amending the agenda to add the proposed noise ordinance.)
>
> The requirements of state law may limit the council's ability to suspend its rules in certain situations. So, for instance, the council may not suspend the rules to add to its agenda action on a proposed amendment to a zoning ordinance unless it has complied with the statutory public notice and hearing requirements that apply to such

---

82. *See generally RONR* (11th ed.) 219, ll. 1–20; 220, ll. 1–35; 221, ll. 1–18 (discussing key features of the call for the orders of the day).

83. *See generally RONR* (11th ed.) § 25, at 260–67 (describing characteristics of the motion to suspend the rules).

measures.[84] Some provisions in these rules incorporate requirements of state law, and therefore may not lawfully be suspended. For example, the council may not suspend the notice requirements for special meetings set out in Rule 10 because they are compulsory under the open meetings law and G.S. 160A-71.

A motion to suspend the rules fails unless it receives affirmative votes equal to at least two-thirds of the council's actual membership, not including vacancies and not counting the mayor if the mayor votes only in the event of a tie. The purpose of this supermajority threshold is to discourage the council from departing from its rules in the ordinary course of business.

Here is an example of how the two-thirds requirement applies in practice. Suppose a five-seat council is considering a motion to suspend its rules. A member's recent death has left the council with only four members, and the mayor votes only in the case of a tie. The two-thirds majority needed to adopt the motion may be calculated as follows:

- 5 (total number of council seats) − 1 (number of vacant seats) = 4.
- $4 \times .666 = 2.664$.
- Because two-thirds of 4 equals a number between 2 and 3, the council must round up to 3, since 2 votes would not satisfy the two-thirds majority requirement. Accordingly, at least 3 votes are necessary to suspend the rules in this scenario.

The motion to suspend the rules is open to abuse, especially on a three-member council, where the two-thirds majority is the same as a simple majority. Two members could readily manipulate the motion to the detriment of the third member. They might, for example, routinely exclude the third member from debate by repeatedly suspending the provision in Motion 9 that entitles every member to speak during debate. To avoid the potential for such abuse, a three-member council could decide to require a unanimous vote for any suspension of the rules.

---

84. *See* G.S. 160A-364 (setting out procedures for adopting, amending, and repealing zoning and other development ordinances). *See also* David Owens, *Mandated Notices in Land Development Regulations*, COATES' CANONS: NC LOC. GOV'T L. BLOG (Jan. 28, 2014), http://canons.sog.unc.edu/mandated-notices-in-land-development-regulations (summarizing the notice requirements that apply to the adoption, amendment, and repeal of development ordinances).

Motion 7. To Divide a Complex Motion. This motion is in order whenever a member wishes to consider and vote on parts of a complex motion separately. The member who makes this motion must specify how the complex motion will be divided.

> **Comment:** This motion can help simplify debate on a complex proposal, particularly when members' support for or opposition to the proposal's component parts is not uniform. Aside from being debatable, it is roughly equivalent to the motion for division of a question in *Robert's*.[85]

Motion 8. To Defer Consideration. The council may defer its consideration of a substantive motion, and any proposed amendments thereto, to an unspecified time. A motion that has been deferred expires unless the council votes to revive it pursuant to Motion 13 within [100] days of deferral. A new motion having the same effect as a deferred motion may not be introduced until the latter has expired.

> **Comment:** This motion is a hybrid of two motions in *Robert's*: the motion to postpone indefinitely and the motion to lay on the table.[86] If adopted, a motion to postpone indefinitely effectively kills the pending substantive motion at which it takes aim, thereby enabling a deliberative body to defeat the substantive motion without actually voting on it.[87] In contrast, a motion to lay on the table allows a deliberative body to set aside a pending substantive motion temporarily when a matter demanding immediate attention arises.[88] The body

---

85. *See generally RONR* (11th ed.) § 27, at 270–76 (discussing main features of the motion for division of a question).

86. *See generally RONR* (11th ed.) § 11, at 126–30 (describing characteristics of the motion to postpone indefinitely); *RONR* (11th ed.) § 17, at 209–18 (setting out the rules that apply to a motion to lay on the table).

87. *RONR* (11th ed.) 126, ll. 4–7 ("*Postpone Indefinitely* is a motion that the assembly decline to take a position on the main question. Its adoption kills the main motion . . . and avoids a direct vote on the question. It is useful in disposing of a badly chosen main motion that cannot be either adopted or expressly rejected without possibly undesirable consequences.").

88. *RONR* (11th ed.) 209, ll. 26–30 ("The motion to *Lay on the Table* enables the assembly to lay the pending question aside temporarily when something else of immediate urgency has arisen or when something else needs to be addressed before consideration of the pending question is resumed. . . .").

may return to the tabled motion later through the adoption of a motion to remove from the table.[89]

Under these rules, the motion to defer consideration is the proper mechanism for killing a substantive motion indirectly or for delaying consideration of it temporarily. If the council's goal is to kill the substantive motion indirectly, it merely has to adopt a deferral motion and leave the substantive motion in limbo until the period during which a motion to revive consideration (Motion 13) would be in order elapses, at which time the substantive motion automatically expires. If the objective is to put off consideration of the substantive motion temporarily, the council may accomplish its goal by adopting a deferral motion and later voting within the prescribed number of days to revive consideration. Like a motion to postpone indefinitely and a motion to table, a motion to defer consideration may include both a pending substantive motion and any pending motions to amend the substantive motion.

In general, the council may not consider a new substantive motion that would have the same effect as a deferred motion until the deadline for reviving the latter has passed. Of course, if the council is determined to take up the new motion while the deferred motion remains pending, it may do so under Motion 6 by voting to suspend its rules to allow consideration of the new motion.

The motion to defer consideration should be distinguished from Motion 10, which may be used to postpone consideration of a substantive motion to a designated time. A substantive motion that has been postponed to a certain time must be brought up again at the time specified. No motion to revive is needed.

Motion 9. To End Debate (Call the Previous Question). If adopted, this motion terminates debate on a pending motion, thereby bringing it to an immediate vote. This motion is not in order until every member has had an opportunity to speak once on the pending motion.

> **Comment:** Many people wrongly assume that a member may bring debate on a pending motion to a close simply by saying, "I call the question," or words to that effect. A body that allows a single member

---

89. *RONR* (11th ed.) 300, ll. 3–5 ("The object of the motion to *Take from the Table* is to make pending again before the assembly a motion or a series of adhering motions that previously has been laid on the table.").

to end debate in that way offends the fundamental parliamentary principle of majority rule. If a majority of members want debate on a matter to continue, no single member should have the power to override their will. Furthermore, allowing a single member to decide when debate must end could infringe on the right of other members to participate equally in the debate.

Under both *Robert's* and these rules, the words "I call the question" amount to a motion to end debate on a pending matter.[90] If a member calls the question when more than one motion is pending, the presiding officer should ensure that the member specifies the motion(s) on which he or she would like debate to stop.

Motion 9 differs from the motion for the previous question in *Robert's* in three significant respects. First, it is debatable.[91] Second, whereas *Robert's* allows a member to call the question at almost any point during a debate, provided the member has been recognized, Motion 8 bars the calling of the question until every member has had a chance to speak at least once.[92] Third, *Robert's* requires a two-thirds majority to bring debate to a close, but a simple majority of votes cast is enough to end debate under these rules.[93]

Motion 10. To Postpone to a Certain Time. This motion may be employed to delay the council's consideration of a substantive motion, and any proposed amendments thereto, until a designated day, meeting, or hour. During the period of postponement, the council may not take up a new motion raising essentially the same issue without first suspending its rules pursuant to Motion 6.

> **Comment:** This motion is similar to the motion to postpone to a certain time (or definitely) in *Robert's*.[94] It allows the council to

---

90. *RONR* (11th ed.) 202, ll. 5-10.

91. *RONR* (11th ed.) 200, l. 1.

92. A member may not interrupt another member to move the previous question. *RONR* (11th ed.) 199, l. 30.

93. *See RONR* (11th ed.) 200, ll. 24–30; 201, ll. 1–2 (noting that *Robert's* imposes a supermajority requirement on the motion for the previous question because otherwise "a temporary majority of only one vote could deny the remaining members all opportunity to discuss any measure that such a majority wished to adopt or kill"). The rationale in *Robert's* for requiring a supermajority to end debate does not apply here because Motion 9 is not in order until every council member has had the opportunity to speak at least once on the motion in question.

94. *See generally RONR* (11th ed.) § 14, at 179–91 (setting out the rules applicable to a motion to postpone to a certain time (or definitely)).

postpone consideration of a matter until a particular day, meeting, or hour. The motion is appropriate when the council needs more information or deliberations on the matter are likely to be lengthy.

This motion should be distinguished from the motion to defer consideration (Motion 8), which can postpone the council's consideration of a matter indefinitely.

Motion 11. To Refer a Motion to a Committee. The council may vote to refer a substantive motion to a committee for study and recommendations. While the substantive motion is pending before the committee, the council may not take up a new motion raising essentially the same issue without first suspending its rules pursuant to Motion 6. If the committee fails to report on the motion within [60] days of the referral date, the council must take up the motion if asked to do so by the member who introduced it.

> **Comment:** The analogous motion in *Robert's* does not grant the introducer of a proposal the power to force consideration of the proposal if the committee to which it has been referred fails to act.[95] By creating such a right, these rules make it harder for other council members to defeat a proposal by sending it to a committee that will just "sit" on it. Of course, if the council does not use committees, this motion is unnecessary.

Motion 12. To Amend.

(a) Germaneness. A motion to amend must concern the same subject matter as the motion it seeks to alter.

> **Comment:** An amendment is germane if it *"in some way involve[s]* the same question that is raised by the motion to which it is applied."[96] An amendment is not germane if it introduces a question that is unrelated to the one posed by the original motion, but "an amendment can be hostile to, or even defeat, the spirit of the original motion and still be germane."[97] Of course, if the intent is to defeat the original motion, the most efficient way to accomplish that objective is to vote against the original motion.

---

95. Under *Robert's*, when a body wishes to take up a matter that it has previously referred to a committee, the adoption of a motion to discharge a committee is usually necessary. *RONR* (11th ed.) 310, ll. 31–33; 311, ll. 1–5.

96. *RONR* (11th ed.) 136, ll. 8–9 (emphasis in original).

97. *RONR* (11th ed.) 136, ll. 17–19.

In *Robert's* a motion to amend by deleting and replacing much or all of the original motion is referred to as a "motion to substitute" and is governed by its own subset of procedures.[98] To avoid confusion, these rules require both major and minor changes to be proposed through a motion to amend.

(b) Limit on Number of Motions to Amend. When a motion to amend is under consideration, a motion to amend the amendment may be made; however, no more than one motion to amend and one motion to amend the amendment may be pending at the same time.

> **Comment:** Consistent with *Robert's*, and to reduce the likelihood of confusion, these rules allow only one motion to amend (primary amendment) and one motion to amend the amendment (secondary amendment) to be pending simultaneously.[99] Such amendments are voted on in reverse order; that is, the secondary amendment is voted on first. Once the secondary amendment has been disposed of, another secondary amendment may be offered. The same is true for primary amendments.[100]

(c) Amendments to Ordinances. Any amendment to a proposed ordinance must be reduced to writing before the vote on the amendment.

> **Comment:** When the amendment in question is to a proposed ordinance, this rule directs that the amendment be put in writing before the council votes on it. One reason for this mandate is that, if the amendment is adopted and the ordinance passes, the amended ordinance may impose legal obligations or restrictions on people, businesses, or other entities inside the city's corporate limits or, in the case of a zoning or other development ordinance, within the city's extraterritorial jurisdiction. It seems prudent to reduce matters of such importance to writing prior to a vote so that council members will fully understand the change(s) they are being asked to make. Additionally, by putting all amendments to proposed ordinances in writing, the council will make it easier for the clerk to produce an accurate final version of the ordinance to be attached to the minutes and filed in the city's ordinance book pursuant to G.S. 160A-78 or

---

98. *RONR* (11th ed.) 153–52.
99. *RONR* (11th ed.) 135, ll. 27–30.
100. *Id.*

incorporated into the city's code of ordinances in accordance with G.S. 160A-77.

If the member who made the original motion disapproves of a pending motion to amend, he or she is free under Rule 24 to withdraw the original motion, so long as no other proposed amendment to the motion has been adopted. If the original motion is withdrawn, another member may put the same issue to the council in the form of a new motion.

Motion 13. To Revive Consideration. The council may vote to revive consideration of any substantive motion that has been deferred pursuant to Motion 8, provided it does so within [100] days of its vote to defer consideration.

> **Comment:** This motion replaces the motion to take from the table in *Robert's*.[101] It has been renamed to make its connection with Motion 8 apparent. Unlike the motion to take from the table, this motion may be debated and amended.[102] If the motion to revive consideration of a deferred motion is not adopted within the prescribed number of days, the deferred motion expires, though at that point the same issue presented by the deferred motion could be reintroduced in the form of a new substantive motion. The number of days specified in Motion 8 and Motion 13 should be the same.

Motion 14. To Reconsider. The council may vote to reconsider its action on a matter, provided the motion to reconsider is made (a) at the same meeting during which the action to be reconsidered was taken and (b) by a member who voted with the prevailing side. For purposes of this motion, "the same meeting" includes any continuation of a meeting through a motion to recess to a certain time and place (Motion 3). The motion is not in order if it interrupts the council's deliberation on a pending matter.

> **Comment:** The restrictions on who may move to reconsider and when a motion to reconsider may be offered correspond to limitations imposed on the parallel motion in *Robert's*.[103]

---

101. *See generally RONR* (11th ed.) § 34, at 300–04 (describing characteristics of the motion to take from the table).

102. *RONR* (11th ed.) 301, ll. 22–23.

103. *RONR* (11th ed.) 315, ll. 28–31; 316, ll. 22–26.

The "prevailing side" is usually the majority, but not always. Some actions require more than a simple majority for approval. (The adoption of a proposed ordinance on the date of introduction under Rule 33 is one example.) If a motion to take such an action garners a simple majority but not the necessary supermajority, the members who voted against the motion constitute the prevailing side, even though they were in the minority.[104] If a motion fails due to a tie vote, the members who voted against the motion are the prevailing side.

The limitation on when a motion to reconsider may be made should not be understood to prevent the council from reversing itself at a subsequent meeting. In general, the council is free to undo an action taken at a prior meeting, except when reversal would violate the law by, for instance, infringing on vested rights or breaching the terms of a valid contract.

The council may reverse an action taken at a previous meeting in either of two ways. It may pass a new motion that has the opposite effect of the one previously adopted. Alternatively, as permitted by Motion 15, the council may vote to rescind or repeal the prior action.

The motion to reconsider is allowed under these rules only when action on a pending matter concludes.

Motion 15. To Rescind. The council may vote to rescind an action taken at a prior meeting provided rescission is not forbidden by law.

> **Comment:** Each meeting of a city council is in many respects a separate legal event. Consequently, and as noted in the *Comment* to Motion 14, a council may at a subsequent meeting undo an action taken at a previous meeting, except when prohibited by law, as when rescission would violate vested rights or result in the breach of a valid contract.
>
> In contrast to a motion to reconsider, a motion to rescind may be made at any time, and by any member, after the meeting at which the action to be reversed was taken.

Motion 16. To Prevent Reintroduction for [Six] Months. This motion may be used to prevent the reintroduction of a failed substantive motion for a time, but it is in order only when made immediately following the

---

104. In its section on motions to reconsider, *Robert's* acknowledges that, when a motion requires a supermajority for adoption, the minority can be the "prevailing side" if the motion fails. *RONR* (11th ed.) 315, ll. 34–36; 316, l. 1.

substantive motion's defeat. To be adopted, this motion must receive votes equal to at least two-thirds of the council's actual membership, excluding vacant seats and not counting the mayor, unless the mayor may vote on all questions. If this motion is adopted, the ban on reintroduction remains in effect for [six] months or until the council's next organizational meeting, whichever occurs first.

> **Comment:** This "clincher" motion can be used to prevent a member from introducing the same motion again and again when the council as a whole has no desire to consider it further. The objection to consideration of a question in *Robert's* serves a similar purpose.[105]
>
> A supermajority is required to adopt this motion because it curtails a member's right to bring a matter before the council. If the council later wishes to take up the matter during the period in which reintroduction is forbidden, it may do so by suspending the rule under Motion 6.
>
> Six months is merely a suggested time; the council may shorten or lengthen the time as it sees fit. In order to give a new council a clean slate, the motion is not effective beyond the council's next organizational meeting.

Part IX. Ordinances and Contracts

Rule 32. Introduction of Ordinances

For purposes of these rules, the "date of introduction" for a proposed ordinance is the date on which the council first votes on the proposed ordinance's subject matter. [The council votes on the subject matter of a proposed ordinance when it votes on whether to adopt or make changes to the proposed ordinance.]

> **Comment:** According to G.S. 160A-75, and as explained in more detail in Rule 33 and the *Comment* thereto, a larger majority is required to adopt a proposed ordinance on the date of introduction than is necessary thereafter. The statute defines "date of introduction" as "the date

---

105. *RONR* (11th ed.) 267, ll. 16–20 ("The purpose of an *Objection to the Consideration of a Question* is to enable the assembly to avoid a particular original main motion altogether when it believes it would be strongly undesirable for the motion even to come before the assembly.").

[on which] the subject matter [of a proposed ordinance] is first voted on by the council." What the statute means by a vote on the subject matter is not specified, and local government attorneys have a range of views on the issue. Some have taken the position that a vote on the subject matter does not happen until the council actually votes on whether to adopt the proposed ordinance. Others have defined "vote on the subject matter" broadly enough to encompass practically any vote related to a proposed ordinance, such as a vote to refer the ordinance to a committee for further study or to set a public hearing on the ordinance. A more conservative approach creates less of a risk that, in a lawsuit challenging the procedures used to adopt an ordinance, the court would find that the council applied the wrong vote requirement because it misperceived what qualifies as the date of introduction. A council that prefers to reduce the risk of such a judicial finding may want to include the bracketed sentence at the end of this rule.

Rule 33. Adoption, Amendment, and Repeal of Ordinances

(a) Adoption of Ordinances.

(1) *Proposed ordinances to be in writing.* No proposed ordinance shall be adopted unless it has been reduced to writing and distributed to members before a vote on adoption is taken.

(2) *Adoption on date of introduction.* To be approved on the date of introduction, a proposed ordinance or any action having the effect of an ordinance must receive affirmative votes equal to at least two-thirds of the council's actual membership, excluding vacant seats and not counting the mayor, unless the mayor has the right to vote on all questions before the council.

(3) *Adoption after date of introduction.* To be approved after the date of introduction, a proposed ordinance or any action having the effect of an ordinance must receive affirmative votes equal to at least a majority of all council members not excused from voting on the matter. In calculating the number of affirmative votes necessary for approval, the council shall count the mayor if he or she votes on all questions. If the mayor votes only in the case of tie, the mayor's vote counts if there is an equal division.

Comment: Paragraph (a) of this rule basically paraphrases the special voting requirements in G.S. 160A-75 for the adoption of ordinances or the taking of any action having the effect of an ordinance. Interestingly, the portion of the statute concerning voting rules for the date of introduction omits any reference to mayors who vote on all questions. Subparagraph (a)(3) assumes that such mayors must be counted as members of the council after the date of introduction, just as they are on the date of introduction.

Voting requirements for ordinance adoption. The different voting requirements that apply to the adoption of a proposed ordinance can be confusing and are perhaps best understood through examples.

Example 1: Vote on date of introduction (two-thirds majority required). The council has seven seats, one of which is vacant. The mayor does not count because he or she does not vote on all questions. The vote on the proposed ordinance is three to two in favor. Whether the number of ayes is sufficient to adopt the proposed ordinance on the date of introduction may be calculated in accordance with subparagraph (a)(2) as follows:

- 7 (total council seats) − 1 (vacant seat) = 6.
- 2/3 of 6 = 4.

Because four affirmative votes were needed to adopt the proposed ordinance on the date of introduction, and it received only three such votes, the council has not adopted the proposed ordinance. This outcome does not necessarily spell the end of the proposed ordinance. The council could take it up at a future meeting, when the less demanding voting requirements in subparagraph (a)(3) would apply.

Example 2: Vote not on date of introduction (simple majority required). The council has six seats with no vacancies. The mayor votes only in case of a tie. One member has been excused from voting. The remaining members vote three to two in support of the proposed ordinance. Whether the number of ayes is enough to adopt the proposed ordinance on a date following the date of introduction may be determined pursuant to subparagraph (a)(3) as follows:

- 6 (total council seats) − 1 (excused member) = 5.
- Simple majority of 5 = 3.

The proposed ordinance has been adopted because it received the three votes needed for adoption under the circumstances.

Significantly, whether a vote on a proposed ordinance happens on the date of introduction affects more than the size of the majority necessary for adoption: it also determines how the requisite majority is calculated. For instance, if the vote on a proposed ordinance occurs on the date of introduction, any vacant council seats must be subtracted from the council's total membership, which has the effect of reducing the number of votes needed to satisfy the requirement for a two-thirds majority. On the other hand, if the vote does not take place on the date of introduction, it may be that vacant seats are not subtracted (the statutory language is not clear on this point). Furthermore, the number of members excused from voting on a proposed ordinance is subtracted from the council's total members if the vote occurs on a date other than the date of introduction, but not if it happens on the date of introduction. It may not seem logical for excusals to factor into majority calculations only on dates other than the date of introduction, or for vacancies to matter only on the date of introduction, but those are the parameters established by statute.

The tables in Appendix C are designed to take the guesswork out of ordinance vote calculations. They collectively set out the number of votes required to adopt a proposed ordinance based on the size of the council, whether the vote occurs on the date of introduction, and other statutorily relevant factors.

(b) Amendment and Repeal of Ordinances. The same voting requirements that govern the adoption of proposed ordinances also apply to the amendment or repeal of an ordinance.

> **Comment:** The voting requirements in G.S. 160A-75 pertain not only to motions to adopt ordinances but also to motions to amend or repeal ordinances. As courts in other states and influential treatises on municipal law have acknowledged, a city council must act by ordinance to amend or repeal an ordinance.[106] Consistent with this

---

106. *See, e.g.,* Cent. Realty Corp. v. Allison, 63 S.E.2d 153, 158 (S.C. 1951) ("Ordinarily, a municipal ordinance cannot be amended or repealed by a mere resolution. To accomplish that result a new ordinance must be passed.") (internal quotation marks omitted); 6 McQuillin Mun. Corp. § 21:13 (3d ed.) ("The general rule is that an ordinance cannot be amended, repealed or suspended by an order or resolution, or other act by a council of less dignity than the ordinance itself. Generally, an ordinance cannot be amended, repealed, or suspended by a resolution.") *See also* Trey Allen, *Repealing Ordinances*, Coates' Canons: NC Loc. Gov't Law Blog (Nov. 13, 2015), http://canons.sog.unc.edu/repealing-ordinances/ (analyzing the law pertaining to ordinance repeal).

principle, the same notice and hearing requirements that govern the adoption of zoning and other development ordinances apply to their amendment or repeal.[107]

Rule 34. Adoption of the Budget Ordinance

(a) Special Rules for the Adoption or Amendment of the Budget Ordinance. Notwithstanding any provision in the city charter, general law, or local act,

(1) the council may adopt or amend the budget ordinance at a regular or special meeting of the council by a simple majority of those members present and voting, a quorum being present;

(2) no action taken with respect to the adoption or amendment of the budget ordinance need be published or is subject to any other procedural requirement governing the adoption of ordinances or resolutions by the council; and

(3) the adoption or amendment of the budget ordinance and the levy of taxes in the budget ordinance are not subject to the provisions of any city charter or local act concerning initiative or referendum.

(b) Notice Requirements for Budget Meetings. During the period beginning with the submission of the budget to the council and ending with the adoption of the budget ordinance, the council may hold any special meetings that may be necessary to complete its work on the budget ordinance. Except for the notice requirements of the open meetings law, which continue to apply, no provision of law concerning the call of special meetings applies during that period so long as

- each member of the board has actual notice of each special meeting called for the purpose of considering the budget and
- no business other than consideration of the budget is taken up.

(c) No Authority for Closed Sessions. This rule shall not be construed to authorize the council to hold closed sessions on any basis other than the grounds set out in Rule 5.

> **Comment:** With minor modifications, this rule restates G.S. 159-17, which creates an exception to ordinance voting requirements for the budget ordinance and budget amendments.

---

107. G.S. 160A-364(a).

Paragraph (b) acknowledges that the notice requirements of the open meeting law apply to meetings held to work on the budget ordinance. It eliminates, however, the need to comply with the provisions in G.S. 160A-71 concerning notice to individual council members so long as each member receives actual notice of any special meeting called to consider the budget.

When more than the initial meeting is necessary to finish the budget ordinance, many councils use one or more recessed meetings to complete their work.

Rule 35. Approval of Contracts and Authorization of Expenditures

(a) Contracts to be in Writing. No contract shall be approved or ratified by the city council unless it has been reduced to writing at the time of the council's vote.

(b) Approval of Contracts. To be approved or ratified, a contract must receive affirmative votes equal to at least a majority of all council members not excused from voting on the contract, including the mayor's vote in the event of a tie.

(c) Authorization of Expenditure of Public Funds. The same vote necessary to approve or ratify a contract is required for the council to authorize the expenditure of public funds, except when the expenditure is authorized pursuant to Rule 34.

> **Comment:** State law mandates that all city contracts be in writing, though it permits the city council to ratify an unwritten contract.[108] Paragraph (a) prevents ratification until the unwritten contract has been reduced to writing.
>
> Under G.S. 160A-75, the same voting requirements that apply to the adoption of a proposed ordinance on a date other than the date of introduction control the approval of contracts. The same is true for a vote authorizing the expenditure of public funds, except when the expenditure is part of the budget ordinance.
>
> Table C.1 in Appendix C sets out the number of affirmative votes necessary for the council to approve a contract based on the total number of members and the number of members excused from voting.

---

108. G.S. 160A-16.

Part X. Public Hearings and Comment Periods

Rule 36. Public Hearings

(a) Calling Public Hearings. In addition to holding public hearings required by law, the council may hold any public hearings it deems advisable. The council may schedule hearings or delegate that responsibility to city staff members, as appropriate, except when state law directs the council itself to call the hearing. If the council delegates scheduling authority, it must provide adequate guidance to assist staff members in exercising that authority.

> **Comment:** Some councils allow staff members to schedule public hearings on the council's behalf. Paragraph (a) sanctions that practice except when otherwise limited by law, but it also requires an explicit delegation of authority by the council and clear guidelines for the exercise of the delegated authority.[109] Courts are often very particular about the procedural requirements for public hearings. It is imperative that the council ensure that staff members follow statutory and any council-established procedures when they schedule public hearings.

(b) Public Hearing Locations. Public hearings may be held anywhere within the city or within the county where the city is located.

> **Comment:** Paragraph (b) restates the geographic limitation on public hearings contained in G.S. 160A-81.

---

109. Numerous state laws mandate that the council hold public hearings prior to taking certain kinds of actions. *See* David M. Lawrence, *When Are Public Hearings Required*, COATES' CANONS: NC LOC. GOV'T L. BLOG (Aug. 21, 2009) http://canons.sog.unc.edu/when-are-public-hearings-required (cataloging city or county actions that trigger statutory public hearing requirements). Most of these statutes direct the council to "hold" a hearing, usually subject to some kind of public notice requirement. *See, e.g.,* 160A-364(a) ("Before adopting, amending, or repealing any ordinance authorized by this Article, the city council shall hold a public hearing on it."). When such a statute is involved, there usually will not be any legal reason why the council may not delegate the scheduling of the hearing to staff. The wording in a few statutes, though, appears to oblige the council itself to set the dates for public hearings on certain topics. Under G.S. 160A-102, for example, if a council wishes to amend the city charter by ordinance, it must first adopt a resolution of intent and, at the same time "call a public hearing on the proposed charter amendments." Similarly, statutory provisions governing voluntary annexations expressly require the council to "fix a date" for an annexation hearing. G.S. 160A-30(c); 160A-58.2.

(c) Rules for Public Hearings. The council may adopt reasonable rules for public hearings that, among other things,

- fix the maximum time allotted to each speaker,
- provide for the designation of spokespersons for groups of persons supporting or opposing the same positions,
- provide for the selection of delegates from groups of persons supporting or opposing the same positions when the number of persons wishing to attend the hearing exceeds the capacity of the hall (so long as arrangements are made, in the case of a hearing subject to the open meetings law, for those excluded from the hall to listen to the hearing), and
- provide for the maintenance of order and decorum in the conduct of the hearing.

> **Comment:** Paragraph (c) incorporates provisions in G.S. 160A-81 regarding rules for public hearings. In keeping with the spirit of the open meetings law, it also dictates that group members desiring to be present at a hearing covered by that law be given the opportunity to listen to the proceedings—outside the meeting room if necessary—if the room is too small to accommodate them.

(d) Notice of Public Hearings. Any public hearing at which a majority of the council is present shall be considered part of a regular or special meeting. Consequently, the relevant notice and related requirements of the open meetings law, as set out in Rules 9 through 12, apply to such hearings. Some statutes mandate additional notice for particular types of hearings, and such notice must be provided together with notice of the meeting during which the hearing will take place.

> **Comment:** A public hearing triggers the notice, minutes, and other requirements of the open meetings law if a majority of the council is present for the hearing, since under those circumstances it qualifies as an official meeting of the council. Depending on the topic of the hearing, other statutory notice requirements also may have to be satisfied.[110]

(e) Continuing Public Hearings. The council may continue any public hearing without further advertisement to a time and place certain, provided the time

---

110. For a list of the various statutes requiring cities to hold public hearings, see Appendix 2 in BLUESTEIN & LAWRENCE, *supra* note 10, at 111–13.

(including the date, if the hearing will resume on a different day) and place of the continued hearing are announced in open session. Except for hearings conducted pursuant to paragraph (g), if a quorum of the council is not present for a properly scheduled public hearing, the hearing must be continued until the council's next regular meeting without further advertisement.

> **Comment:** Paragraph (e) essentially restates provisions in G.S. 160A-81 on continuing hearings.

(f) Conduct of Public Hearings. At the time appointed for the hearing, the mayor shall call the hearing to order and proceed to allow public input in accordance with any rules adopted by the council for the hearing. Unless the council extends the hearing, when the time allotted for the hearing expires, or when no one wishes to speak who has not done so, the mayor shall [declare the hearing closed] [entertain a motion to close the hearing], and the council shall resume the regular order of business.

> **Comment:** Some councils allow the mayor to close a public hearing, while others require a motion and vote. Either practice is acceptable, as indicated by the optional language in brackets.

(g) Public Hearings by Less Than a Majority of Council Members. Nothing in this rule prevents the council from appointing a member or members to hold a public hearing on the council's behalf, except when state law requires that the council itself conduct the hearing.

> **Comment:** By providing that a public hearing is deferred until the council's next regular meeting if a quorum is not present at the scheduled time, G.S. 160A-81 might appear to imply that a quorum is necessary for any public hearing scheduled by the council. Rightly understood, however, the statute concerns public hearings mandated by law, as well as discretionary public hearings that the council decides to conduct as a body. There is no legal reason why the council could not appoint one or more members short of a quorum to conduct a public hearing that is not required by law, and some-times good reason exists for doing so. Suppose, for example, that the council wants public input on a controversial proposal to cap the number of dogs or cats per residence. Inasmuch as no statute directs the council to hold a public hearing prior to adopting such an ordinance, the council could decide to have individual members conduct hearings throughout the city in order to capture a broader sample of public opinion.

When the council authorizes more than one member to conduct a public hearing not required by law, the safe course of action with regard to the open meetings law is to assume that the members tasked with holding the hearing constitute a committee of the council and that the hearing is therefore subject to the law's public notice and related requirements for special meetings.

Rule 37. Public Comment Periods

(a) Frequency of Public Comment Periods. The council must provide at least one opportunity for public comment each month at a regular meeting, except that the council need not offer a public comment period during any month in which it does not hold a regular meeting.

(b) Rules for Public Comment Periods. The council may adopt reasonable rules for public comment periods that, among other things,

- fix the maximum time allotted to each speaker,
- provide for the designation of spokespersons for groups supporting or opposing the same positions,
- provide for the selection of delegates from groups supporting or opposing the same positions when the number of persons wishing to attend the public comment period exceeds the capacity of the hall (so long as arrangements are made for those excluded from the hall to listen to the hearing), and
- provide for the maintenance of order and decorum in the conduct of the hearing.

(c) Content-Based Restrictions Generally Prohibited. The council may not restrict speakers based on subject matter, as long as their comments pertain to subjects within the council's real or apparent jurisdiction.

> **Comment:** Paragraphs (a) and (b) largely paraphrase G.S. 160A-81.1. In keeping with the spirit of the open meetings law, paragraph (b) likewise requires that all group members desiring to be present for the public comment period be given the opportunity to listen to the proceedings—outside the meeting room if necessary—if the room is too small to accommodate them.
>
> Paragraph (c) recognizes that the free speech guarantee in the First Amendment to the United States Constitution applies to public comment periods. Specifically, in First Amendment jargon, the public comment period constitutes a "limited public forum," which means

that the council may impose reasonable time, place, and manner restrictions. Restrictions premised on the content or viewpoint of a speaker's remarks will usually be deemed unconstitutional, though the council probably may insist that speakers confine their statements to matters related in some way to matter's within the council's real or apparent jurisdiction.[111]

Part XI. Appointments and Appointed Bodies

Rule 38. Appointments

(a) **Appointments in Open Session.** The council must consider and make any appointment to another body or, in the event of a vacancy on the council, to its own membership in open session.

> **Comment:** The open meetings law expressly prohibits a public body from meeting in closed session to consider or make appointments to other public bodies.[112] It also forbids a public body from meeting in closed session to consider or fill a vacancy among its own membership.[113]

(b) **Nomination and Voting Procedure.** The council shall use the following procedure to fill a vacancy in the council itself or in any other body over which it has the power of appointment. [The nominating committee shall be called upon to make its report and recommendation(s), if any.] The mayor shall [then] open the floor for nominations, whereupon council members may put forward and debate nominees. When debate ends, the mayor shall call the roll of the members, and each member shall cast a vote for his or her preferred nominee. The voting shall continue until a nominee receives a majority of votes cast during a single balloting.

> **Comment:** This rule recommends that the council make appointments through a nomination procedure. An alternative way of proceeding is by motion. A member moves that the council appoint

---

111. For an overview of constitutional limitations on the authority of local governments to control statements made during public comment periods, see Frayda S. Bluestein, *Public Comment Period Policies: What's Legal?* Coates' Canons: NC Loc. Gov't L. Blog (Mar. 15, 2016), http://canons.sog.unc.edu/public-comment-period-policies-whats-legal.

112. G.S. 143-318.11(a)(6).

113. *Id.*

an individual, and following debate, the council votes on the motion. If the motion passes, the seat is filled. If it fails, the floor is then open to a new motion. One downside to the appointment-by-motion method is that it puts members who prefer other candidates in the uncomfortable position of having to vote against the person named in the motion. The nomination procedure allows each member to vote for his or her preferred candidate without having to vote against anyone else.

As implied by the optional language in brackets, several councils use nominating committees to consider and recommend appointments. It is likewise quite common for councils to solicit applications for appointment from citizens.

(c) Mayor. The mayor may [not] make nominations [or][and] vote on appointments under this rule.

> **Comment:** A council that adopts this rule should include the words "not" and "or" in paragraph (c) unless its mayor has the right to vote on all questions. As noted in the *Comment* to Rule 17(b), many mayors have the right to vote only when an equal number of affirmative and negative votes have been cast. If a council uses the appointment-by-motion method, members vote "aye" or "no" on a motion to appoint a specific individual, and a mayor who may vote only in the event of a tie is able to break any deadlock. Under the nomination procedure prescribed by this rule, however, members do not cast "aye" or "no" votes, so a mayor who may vote only in case of a tie does not vote at all. On the other hand, if a mayor is entitled to vote on all questions before the council, he or she has the same right to vote on appointments as any member of the council.
>
> As with the ability to offer motions, the mayor's voting status should control whether the mayor may nominate individuals under this rule to fill vacancies on the council or on appointed boards for which the council has the power of appointment. A mayor with the right to vote on all questions should have the same ability to nominate as any council member. A mayor who votes only in the event of a tie, and who for that reason may not vote on nominations under this rule, should not make nominations.

(d) Multiple Appointments. If the council is filling more than one vacancy, each member shall have as many votes in each balloting as there are slots to be filled, and the votes of a majority of the total number of members voting shall be required for each appointment. No member may cast more than one vote for the same candidate for the same vacancy during a single balloting.

> **Comment:** Paragraph (d) explains how the procedures set out in paragraph (b) work when more than one appointment is being made.

(e) Duty to Vote. It is the duty of each member to vote for as many appointees as there are appointments to be made, but failure to do so shall not invalidate a member's ballot.

> **Comment:** As explained in the *Comment* to Rule 28, the law obliges members to vote on all questions that come before the council, except when a member has been excused for a legally sufficient reason. The usual consequence of a member's unexcused failure to vote is that the member is recorded as having voted in the affirmative. Yet because members do not vote "aye" or "no" when voting on proposed appointments under this rule, it would not make sense to record a member's unexcused failure to vote as an affirmative vote. Accordingly, when multiple appointments are being made, a member's failure to vote on one or more of the appointments will not invalidate the member's votes on the remaining appointments. Although the council might wish to impose such a consequence for non-voting, it may not have statutory authority to do so.

(f) Vote by Written Ballot. The council may vote on proposed appointments by written ballot in accordance with Rule 29.

> **Comment:** Written ballots may also be used if the council employs the appointment-by-motion method.

Rule 39. Committees and Boards

(a) Establishment and Appointment. The council may establish temporary and standing committees, boards, and other bodies to help carry on the work of city government. Unless otherwise provided by law or the council, the power of appointment to such bodies lies with the council.

> **Comment:** With certain limitations, the city council has broad authority to "create, change, abolish, and consolidate offices, positions, departments, boards, commissions, and agencies of the city government . . . in order to promote [the] orderly and efficient administration of city affairs."[114] For the most part, the power to

---

114. G.S. 160A-146.

make appointments to city bodies belongs to the council, though many councils delegate that power to their mayors. The sole board the mayor has statutory power to appoint is the housing authority.[115]

(b) Open Meetings Law. The requirements of the open meetings law apply whenever a majority of an appointed body's members gather in person or simultaneously by electronic means to discuss or conduct official business. They do not apply to meetings solely among the city's professional staff.

> **Comment:** Official meetings of a city's appointed bodies, like those of council, trigger the notice, access, and related requirements of the open meetings law. (This is so regardless of whether the body is labeled a committee, board, commission, or some other term.) Yet as the law itself recognizes, meetings consisting merely of a city's professional staff do not.[116]

(c) Procedural Rules. The council may prescribe the procedures by which the city's appointed bodies operate, subject to any statutory provisions applicable to particular bodies. [In the absence of rules adopted by the council, an appointed body may promulgate its own procedural rules, so long as they are in keeping with any relevant statutory provisions and generally accepted principles of parliamentary procedure.]

> **Comment:** Specific statutes govern the functioning of some appointed bodies. Boards of adjustment, for example, must operate in accordance with statutory provisions that regulate how they conduct business.[117]
>
> As the creator of the city's appointed bodies, the council has the power to determine the rules under which they will function, except when the rules are set by state law. It often happens, though, that the council will neglect to adopt procedural rules for its appointed bodies, thereby increasing the odds that meetings of those bodies will be marked by confusion. (Without procedural rules, for instance, how does an appointed body know whether to include vacant seats in its quorum calculations? The relationship between vacant seats and quorum determinations is not addressed in *Robert's Rules of Order*.)

---

115. G.S. 157-5.

116. G.S. 143-318.10(c).

117. *See, e.g.*, David W. Owens, Land Use Law in North Carolina 143–58 (2nd ed. 2011) (describing the procedures that a board of adjustment must follow when conducting quasi-judicial proceedings).

The optional language in brackets strives to obviate this problem by authorizing appointed bodies to adopt their own procedural rules if the council leaves them to their own devices.

Part XII. Miscellaneous

Rule 40. Amendment of the Rules

These rules may be amended at any regular meeting or at any properly called special meeting for which amendment of the rules is one of the meeting's stated purposes. Any amendment to these rules must be consistent with the city charter, any relevant statutes, and generally accepted principles of parliamentary procedure. To be adopted, a motion to amend these rules must be approved by a majority of the council's members, excluding vacant seats and counting the mayor only if the mayor may vote on all questions.

> **Comment:** As remarked in the *Comment* to Rule 1, the council has broad authority to adopt procedural rules that do not conflict with its charter provisions, state statutes, or generally accepted principles of parliamentary procedure. That same authority extends to the amendment of such rules.
>
> An actual majority of council members, rather than a simple majority of votes cast, is necessary to approve proposed amendments to these rules. Without this requirement, a minority of the members might be tempted to alter these rules when other members are absent to allow for some action disfavored by most of their colleagues. Rule 40 should not be confused with a motion to suspend the rules under Rule 31, Motion 6

Rule 41. Reference to *Robert's Rules of Order Newly Revised*

The council shall refer to *Robert's Rules of Order Newly Revised* for guidance when confronted with a procedural issue not covered by these rules or state law. Having consulted *Robert's*, the mayor shall make a ruling on the issue subject to appeal to the council under Rule 31, Motion 1.

> **Comment:** Because *Robert's* was written chiefly with large assemblies in mind, many of its provisions may not be ideal for a small board. Except insofar as they embody general principles of parliamentary procedure, those provisions should be viewed as purely advisory in nature. They do not bind the council.

Appendix A. Quorum for a City Council

Table A1. Number of Members Needed for a Quorum

Total Number of Council Seats, Plus Mayor	Number of Vacant Seats												
	0	1	2	3	4	5	6	7	8	9	10	11	12
4	3	2	2	—	—	—	—	—	—	—	—	—	—
5	3	3	2	2	—	—	—	—	—	—	—	—	—
6	4	3	3	2	2	—	—	—	—	—	—	—	—
7	4	4	3	3	2	2	—	—	—	—	—	—	—
8	5	4	4	3	3	2	2	—	—	—	—	—	—
9	5	5	4	4	3	3	2	2	—	—	—	—	—
10	6	5	5	4	4	3	3	2	2	—	—	—	—
11	6	6	5	5	4	4	3	3	2	2	—	—	—
12	7	6	6	5	5	4	4	3	3	2	2	—	—
13	7	7	6	6	5	5	4	4	3	3	2	2	—

Appendix B. Order of Precedence for Procedural Motions

Motion	Vote Required*	Notes
To appeal a procedural ruling of the presiding officer	Majority	This motion is in order immediately after the ruling being appealed and at no other time. The member making the motion need not be recognized, and, if timely, the motion may not be ruled out of order.
To adjourn	Majority	None
To recess to a time and place certain	Majority	This motion must state the time (including the date, if the meeting will reconvene on a different day) and place at which the meeting will resume.
To take a brief recess	Majority	The presiding officer may call a brief recess at any time on his or her own authority.
To follow the agenda	Majority	This motion must be made when an item of business that deviates from the agenda is proposed or it is out of order as to that item.
To suspend the rules	Two-thirds	The council may not suspend provisions that incorporate state law.
To divide a complex motion	Majority	None
To defer consideration	Majority	This motion is a hybrid of the traditional motion to postpone indefinitely and the motion to lay on the table. A substantive motion that is deferred expires [100] days after the deferral date unless a timely motion to revive consideration (Motion 13) is adopted. While a deferred motion remains pending, a new motion with the same effect may not be introduced unless the council first votes to suspend its rules (Motion 6).
To end debate ("call the previous question")	Majority	Any substantive or procedural motion is potentially subject to a motion to end debate. A motion to end debate on a pending motion is not in order until every member has had a chance to speak once.

Motion	Vote Required*	Notes
To postpone to a certain time	Majority	This motion may be used to delay consideration of a substantive motion until a designated day, meeting, or hour. While a postponed motion remains pending, a new motion with the same effect may not be introduced unless the council first votes to suspend its rules (Motion 6).
To refer a motion to a committee	Majority	If the committee fails to report on the motion within [60] days, the council must take up the referred motion again at the request of the member who introduced it. During the referral period, a substantive motion with the same effect may not be introduced unless the council first votes to suspend its rules (Motion 6).
To amend	Majority	Any substantive or any procedural motion other than a motion to appeal (Motion 1) may be amended. A motion to amend must concern the same subject matter as the motion that it seeks to alter. No more than one motion to amend and one motion to amend the amendment may be pending at the same time. Any amendment to a proposed ordinance must be reduced to writing before the vote on the amendment.
To revive consideration	Majority	This motion is in order within [100] days of the vote to defer consideration (Motion 8).
To reconsider	Majority	To be in order, this motion must be made by a member of the prevailing side at the same meeting during which the original vote was taken. The motion may not interrupt deliberation on a pending matter.
To rescind	Majority	This motion is not in order if rescission is forbidden by law.
To prevent reintroduction	Two-thirds	This motion is in order immediately following the defeat of a substantive motion and at no other time. If adopted, it bars the reintroduction of the failed substantive motion for [six] months or until the council's next organizational meeting, whichever comes first. If the council wishes to take up the substantive motion during the period in which reintroduction is forbidden, it must first vote to suspend its rules (Motion 6).

Note: This chart is a modified version of one originally created by A. Fleming Bell, II. Under these rules, all procedural motions are debatable, and none requires a second.

*The term "majority" means more than half of votes cast, a quorum being present. The term "two-thirds" refers to two-thirds of the council's actual membership, excluding vacant seats and not counting the mayor unless he or she may vote on all questions.

Appendix C. Number of Votes Required to Adopt an Ordinance or Approve a Contract

Table C1. Number of Votes Needed to Adopt an Ordinance Not on the Date of Introduction or to Approve a Contract

Total Number of Council Members*	Number of Members Excused from Voting												
	0	1	2	3	4	5	6	7	8	9	10	11	12
3	2	2	–	–	–	–	–	–	–	–	–	–	–
4	3	2	2	–	–	–	–	–	–	–	–	–	–
5	3	3	2	2	–	–	–	–	–	–	–	–	–
6	4	3	3	2	2	–	–	–	–	–	–	–	–
7	4	4	3	3	2	2	–	–	–	–	–	–	–
8	5	4	4	3	3	2	2	–	–	–	–	–	–
9	5	5	4	4	3	3	2	2	–	–	–	–	–
10	6	5	5	4	4	3	3	2	2	–	–	–	–
11	6	6	5	5	4	4	3	3	2	2	–	–	–
12	7	6	6	5	5	4	4	3	3	2	2	–	–
13	7	7	6	6	5	5	4	4	3	3	2	2	–

*Include the mayor if he or she votes on all questions or if there is a tie and the mayor breaks the tie.

Table C2. Number of Votes Needed to Adopt an Ordinance on the Date of Introduction (Mayor Votes on All Questions)

Total Number of Council Members, Including Mayor	Number of Vacant Seats												
	0	1	2	3	4	5	6	7	8	9	10	11	12
4	3	2	2	–	–	–	–	–	–	–	–	–	–
5	4	3	2	2	–	–	–	–	–	–	–	–	–
6	4	4	3	2	2	–	–	–	–	–	–	–	–
7	5	4	4	3	2	2	–	–	–	–	–	–	–
8	6	5	4	4	3	2	2	–	–	–	–	–	–
9	6	6	5	4	4	3	2	2	–	–	–	–	–
10	7	6	6	5	4	4	3	2	2	–	–	–	–
11	8	7	6	6	5	4	4	3	2	2	–	–	–
12	8	8	7	6	6	5	4	4	3	2	2	–	–
13	9	8	8	7	6	6	5	4	4	3	2	2	–

Table C3. Number of Votes Needed to Adopt an Ordinance on the Date of Introduction (Mayor Votes Only in Case of a Tie Vote)

Total Number of Council Members, Excluding Mayor	Number of Vacant Seats												
	0	1	2	3	4	5	6	7	8	9	10	11	12
3	2	2	–	–	–	–	–	–	–	–	–	–	–
4	3	2	2	–	–	–	–	–	–	–	–	–	–
5	4	3	2	2	–	–	–	–	–	–	–	–	–
6	4	4	3	2	2	–	–	–	–	–	–	–	–
7	5	4	4	3	2	2	–	–	–	–	–	–	–
8	6	5	4	4	3	2	2	–	–	–	–	–	–
9	6	6	5	4	4	3	2	2	–	–	–	–	–
10	7	6	6	5	4	4	3	2	2	–	–	–	–
11	8	7	6	6	5	4	4	3	2	2	–	–	–
12	8	8	7	6	6	5	4	4	3	2	2	–	–

Appendix D. N.C. City Council Procedures: Selected Statutes

Following are selected North Carolina General Statutes (G.S.) that impose procedural requirements on city councils.

Topic	Statutes(s)
Board structure	G.S. 160A-66, 160A-101 through 111
Board vacancies	G.S. 160A-63
Chairman / Mayor role	G.S. 160A-69, -70
Ethics codes, training	G.S. 160A-86, -87
Meetings—types of meetings	G.S. 160A-68, -71; G.S. 143-318.12, -318.13
Meetings—open meetings requirements	G.S. Chapter 143, Article 33C
Meetings—location, notice	G.S. 160A-71; G.S. 143-318.12, -318.13
Meetings—disruptions	G.S. 143-318.17
Minutes	G.S. 160A-72; G.S. 143-318.10(e)
Ordinance adoption	G.S. 160A-76
Ordinance book and code	G.S. 160A-77, -78, -79
Public hearings	G.S. 160A-81
Public comment periods	G.S. 160A-81.1
Quorum	G.S. 160A-74
Rules of procedure	G.S. 160A-71(c)
Voting	G.S. 160A-69, -70, -75; G.S. 143-318.13

Note: The above chart was prepared by Norma R. Houston, a faculty member at the School of Government.